Reason and Religion

REASON AND RELIGION

Essays in Philosophical Theology

Anthony Kenny

Basil Blackwell

First published 1987

Basil Blackwell Ltd
108 Cowley Road, Oxford, OX4 1JF, UK

Basil Blackwell Inc.
432 Park Avenue South, Suite 1503
New York, NY 10016, USA

British Library Cataloguing in Publication Data
Kenny, Anthony
Reason and religion: essays in philosophical
theology.
1. Philosophical theology
I. Title
230'.01   BT40
ISBN 0–631–15268–7

Library of Congress Cataloging-in-Publication Data

Kenny, Anthony John Patrick,
    Reason and religion.

    Includes index.
    1. Philosophical theology.   I. Title.
BT40.K46   1987   200'.1   86–31709
ISBN 0–631–15268–7

Typeset in 11 on 13 pt Baskerville
by Cambrian Typesetters, Frimley, Surrey
Printed in Great Britain by
T. J. Press Ltd, Padstow

Contents

Contents

Preface

In this volume I have collected papers which I have written on topics of philosophical theology during the last thirty years. Some of them were written while I was a Catholic and a priest; others belong to more recent periods since I have been at a distance from Catholic thought and practice. For this reason I thought of entitling the collection 'Essays Catholic and Critical'. But having re-read the papers I decided that this title would imply a false antithesis. For some of the essays which I wrote as a Catholic are very critical of Catholic doctrine in that they present in sharp relief difficulties and inconsistencies in Catholic teaching; while some of the most recent essays, written from the viewpoint of an agnostic, are more sympathetic to traditional Catholic doctrine than to the prevailing climate of liberal secular opinion.

The essays are all essays in philosophical theology: that is to say, they exhibit the application of philosophical methods to theological topics. Not all of the essays concern what used to be called 'natural theology', namely, truths in the religious sphere allegedly attainable by the unaided use of reason. Several of them are concerned with 'revealed theology', that is to say, they are philosophical examinations of the coherence of doctrines put forward by their proponents on the basis of a particular religious tradition and claimed to be part of the content of divine revelation. All of them can be considered as essays in the philosophy of religion, if that expression is given a broad interpretation.

I have grouped the essays by subject matter, not chronologically.

The essays in the first section, however, both date from the 1960s. They concern issues of theological method, and the relationship between theology, philosophy and logic. The first, which was read to a symposium at Downside Abbey on 'Theology and the University', was published in the proceedings of the symposium under that title by Darton, Longman and Todd in 1964. It summarizes the relationship between analytic philosophy and the philosophy of religion at that period, and applies methods of linguistic analysis to the Catholic doctrine of transubstantiation in a way which brings out the difficulties in stating it coherently. The second paper, 'The development of ecclesiastical doctrine' was read to a conference of Catholic philosophers at Spode House in 1963, and has not hitherto been published. It outlines the difficulties in reconciling the historical data concerning the variations between Church teaching at different periods, and the Catholic doctrine that the Christian revelation was completed before the death of the last of Christ's original apostles.

The second section of the book treats of the nature and existence of God, with particular reference to the proofs that have been offered of his existence. These fall into three main classes: ontological arguments, or arguments from the concept of divinity considered by itself; cosmological arguments, based on features of the universe in which we live, with its features of stability and mutability, its relationships of cause and effect, and its population of goal-directed agents; and empiricist arguments, based on the religious experiences claimed by individuals. At the present time ontological arguments are perhaps the most favoured by religious-minded philosophers; twenty years ago things were very different, and the first two essays in this section aim to show that belief that God is a necessary being does not involve any acceptance of the ontological argument which was then almost universally believed to be a gross fallacy. 'God and Necessity', which included a survey of recent writing on the topic within the analytic tradition, was a contribution to *British Analytical Philosophy* edited by Bernard Williams and Alan Montefiore, published by Routledge and Kegan Paul in 1966. 'Necessary Being', an examination of the kind of necessity attributed to God within the scholastic tradition, was published in the journal *Sophia* in 1962. The third article in the section, which is also the most recent, is an examination of the argument from design which appears to me to be the most persuasive of the cosmological arguments for the existence of God. It has not previously been published. The fourth article concerns the empiricist argument for God's existence: it takes the notion of religious experience in one of its most highly sophisticated forms – the mystical experiences described by St John of the Cross – and tries to show the difficulties latent in the concept of religious experience of this kind. This, though written in 1963, appears here for the first time.

The third section of the book contains three essays devoted to the relationship between divine power and human freedom. The topic of freedom and determinism has always been the most central concern of my philosophical interests. In my book *The God of the Philosophers* (Oxford, 1979) I argued that reflection on these topics provides one of the strongest arguments against the existence of God as traditionally conceived. If God is to have infallible knowledge of future human actions, then determinism must be true. If God is to escape responsibility for human wickedness, then determinism must be false. Hence, I argued in that book, in the notion of a God who foresees all sins but is the author of none there lurks a contradiction. The essays in the present book consider three ways in which Christian authors have sought to disarm the antinomy between God's power and man's freedom. St John Chrysostom made room for human freedom and initiative in the quest for salvation by constricting the role of divine grace in a way which would have been thought heretical in Western thought in the tradition of Augustine. I describe his thought on the topic in the earliest paper of this collection, reprinted in an abbreviated form from the essay 'Was St John Chrysostom a Semi-Pelagian?' in the *Irish Theological Quarterly* for 1958. St Thomas Aquinas accepted that if God necessarily knew all our future actions, those actions must be necessary; he attempted to defuse any threat to human freedom by saying that God's knowledge was not foreknowledge, but was located in eternity outside time. In the second essay of Part III 'Aquinas on divine foreknowledge and freedom' I argue that this position is untenable, but maintain that there is no reason to deny that God's knowledge of the future is contingent. Later, I have come to believe that this does not provide any line of escape from the contradiction between divine foreknowledge and freedom as conceived by the libertarian. A different and highly ingenious line of escape was explored a century after Aquinas by John Wyclif, who maintained that human beings' present and future actions had, in a certain sense, power to affect God's past knowledge. This is the topic of the final essay in the section. Chapter 8 first appeared in a collection of critical essays on Aquinas published by Doubleday in 1969; chapter 9 was read to a Wyclif centenary conference in Oxford in 1985 and will be published in the proceedings of that conference.

The two essays in the final section concern the frontiers between religion and morality. Arguments concerning the morality of abortion are almost always intertwined with the pros and cons of particular religious world-views. In chapter 10 I argue that though a judgement about the permissibility of abortion does presuppose a metaphysical judgement about the identity and nature of the foetus, it is possible to separate the metaphysical issue from the religious one. This paper, which is the most recent in the collection, is in a collection of papers on bioethics presented at King's College, London, entitled *Medicine in Contemporary Society: King's College Studies* (1986–7). The final paper was a public lecture, the Daweid Azfar memorial lecture, delivered before an invited audience in Karachi, in 1985. It concerns the relationship between religion and the state and was invited as a Western contribution to the lively debate in Pakistan on the role of religious tradition within a modern Islamic state.

ANTHONY KENNY

I

The Nature of Theological Thinking

1

The Use of Logical Analysis in Theology

British philosophy today seems ill-fitted to play handmaid to theology. In an age in which most professional philosophers are atheists and few theologians are conversant with professional philosophy there appears little hope of cooperation between the two disciplines even on terms of equality. Yet the gulf of incomprehension between them is not as great as it was thirty years ago. In the thirties the philosophers of the tradition now dominant in England were, for the most part, both ignorant and contemptuous of systematic theology. One of the most brilliant of them, Frank Ramsey, summed up their attitude in a notorious remark. 'Theology and Absolute Ethics,' he wrote, 'are two famous subjects which we have realized to have no real objects.'

In 1936, Professor A. J. Ayer dismissed theology in six pages of his book *Language, Truth and Logic* (London, 1936). According to Ayer there was no way of proving that the existence of a God, such as the God of Christianity, was even probable. When a Christian speaks of God, he intends to talk about a transcendent being which cannot be defined in terms of any empirical manifestations. Therefore, said Ayer, the word 'God' was a metaphysical and meaningless term. 'No sentence,' he concluded, 'which purports to describe the nature of a transcendent God can possess any literal significance.' (*Language, Truth and Logic*, p. 115.)

The philosophy presented in *Language, Truth and Logic* was called by its author 'logical empiricism'. 'The views which are put forward in this treatise,' he wrote, 'derive from the doctrines of

Bertrand Russell and Wittgenstein, which are themselves the logical outcome of the empiricism of Berkeley and David Hume.' Ayer accepted the central doctrine of empiricism, which is that all our knowledge derives from sense-impressions. But he restated this doctrine as a theory of meaning. A word is meaningful, according to *Language, Truth and Logic*, only if it is possible to give rules for translating any sentence in which it may occur into a sentence which refers to sense-contents. Into this restatement of empiricism Ayer incorporated many elements which he had taken from the writings of Russell. Ayer was wrong in regarding Wittgenstein's *Tractatus Logico-Philosophicus* (London, 1922) as an empiricist treatise; but he did find there one doctrine very congenial to empiricism. This was the thesis that all the necessary truths of logic and mathematics were tautologies. Earlier empiricists had argued implausibly that mathematical propositions were open to refutation by experience. Ayer felt himself able to preserve the necessary nature of mathematical truth without infidelity to his empiricist principles, because he asserted that the necessity of such truths was guaranteed solely by our conventions concerning the symbols used to express them. It was for these reasons that Ayer described his version of empiricism as 'logical empiricism'.

In recent years there have been several attempts to present an account of religious belief which would be compatible with some form of logical empiricism. Such attempts may be found in some of the contributions to the symposia *New Essays in Philosophical Theology* (London, 1955) and *Faith and Logic* (London, 1957). Two of the best-known attempts of this kind are Professor I. T. Ramsey's *Religious Language* (London, 1957) and Professor Braithwaite's *An Empiricist's View of the Nature of Religious Belief* (Cambridge, 1955). One of the most recent is John Wilson's book *Philosophy and Religion* (Oxford, 1964). In that book it is suggested that religious assertions about the supernatural are factual assertions which are verified by religious experience in the way in which statements about physical objects are verified by sense-experience. A statement such as 'there is a God', Wilson suggests, means that certain experiences of vital interest and importance are permanently available at least to certain people under certain conditions. In this way, the word 'God' would be made to conform more or less to the conditions of meaningfulness laid down in *Language, Truth and Logic*. Rules would be given for translating any sentence in which it occurred into a sentence which referred only to sense-impressions, though these would be impressions of an inner and mysterious sense, rather than of sight or hearing or touch.

Attempts to reconcile theism with empiricism seem to me misguided. If I suggest that philosophy and theology are less far apart than they were it is not because I hope for success in any such attempt. Professor Ayer seems to me quite correct in believing that the philosophy which he inherited from Hume is incompatible with any theology worthy of the name.

However, since *Language, Truth and Logic* was first published, the philosophy of logical empiricism has been shown to be untenable by thinkers holding no brief for theology. That philosophy, we have seen, contained two major theses. The first was a logical one, that all the truths of logic and mathematics are tautologies. This thesis was refuted by the work of formal logicians in the 1930s, who showed the discontinuity between those parts of logic (such as the propositional calculus) in which the validity of formulae can be checked by mechanical tests and those other parts (including many parts necessary for the formalization of mathematics) for which no such decision procedure is possible. The second thesis was the epistemological thesis that all our knowledge begins with sense-impressions, restated as the theory that only those sentences are meaningful which admit of restatement into sentences referring only to sense-contents. This thesis was refuted by the later work of Wittgenstein, who showed in his posthumously published *Philosophical Investigations* (Oxford, 1953) that the notion of a sense-content, conceived by empiricists as an essentially private and incommunicable entity, was itself a radically incoherent one. To say this, of course, is to take sides in a dispute that is not yet over. But many philosophers in this country and the United States would agree with Alasdair MacIntyre's judgement: 'Wittgenstein's philosophy renders empiricism no longer viable.' (*The New Statesman*, 2 April 1960, p. 491.)

The decline of empiricism must not be seen as a victory for its traditional opponents, idealism and rationalism. Wittgenstein's arguments, if they are valid against Hume's impressions, are equally valid against Descartes's *pensées*. The *Philosophical Investiga-tions* contains little comfort for those theists who seek to establish the existence of God by appeal to an intuition of Being, or who find proof of the immortality of the soul in the contemplation of their own Cartesian ego. Those who accept the conclusions which Wittgenstein reached towards the end of his life are committed to the belief that modern epistemology since Descartes has rested on a very fundamental misconception. Professor Ryle's book *The Concept of Mind* (London, 1949) is a well-known attack on Cartesianism which has enjoyed great influence in this country since the war. One philosopher summed up his deep dissatisfaction with post-Renaissance epistemology in the slogan: 'Back to Aristotle'!

Certainly it is possible to find in several recent philosophical publications evidence of a quickening interest in Aristotelian ideas. Three examples which have appeared in the last few years are Miss Anscombe's *Intention* (Oxford, 1951), Professor Hampshire's *Thought and Action* (London, 1959), and Professor von Wright's *The Varieties of Goodness* (London, 1963). This is no doubt partly due to the fact that Oxford has since the war replaced Cambridge as the centre of philosophical activity in England. Oxford, unlike Cambridge, has long had a tradition of Aristotelian scholarship of the kind illustriously exemplified in the work of Sir David Ross. But Aristotle appears to be taken seriously now by philosophers as well as by historians of philosophy in a way which contrasts sharply with the attitude, say, of Russell and his immediate followers.

Interest in Aristotle's medieval successors has been stimulated from a different quarter. The great advances which have been made during the last 100 years in formal logic were made largely in ignorance of the work done in this field in the Middle Ages. Recently, however, logicians have come to appreciate the achieve-ments of their medieval predecessors. Recent writers have studied in particular the medieval work on questions of modal logic and tense-logic, which is often discarded as sterile by neo-scholastics. (For references see Prior, *Formal Logic* (Oxford, 1959) and *Time and Modality* (Oxford, 1957); Geach, *Reference and Generality* (London, 1962); Kneale, *The Development of Logic* (Oxford, 1962).

It is, no doubt, a contingent fact that much of systematic theology was worked out by thinkers trained in Aristotelian philosophy. But given this historical fact, the circumstances I have mentioned are of significance for the relationship between theology and philosophy. The decay of empiricism has weakened one of the greatest *a priori* obstacles to the construction of a natural theology; the revival of interest in scholastic writings and terminology lessens one of the great practical difficulties in communication between professional philosophers and professional theologians. The renaissance of formal logic has placed within the bounds of possibility a philosophical theology more rigorous than any known to the Middle Ages. But this possibility has not yet been explored. The interests of logicians have been hitherto almost entirely mathematical; only recently has attention been turned to modal and epistemic logic and tense-logics. Yet such branches of logic are important for an assessment of the validity of proofs for the existence of God and for the consideration of the classic problems about his omniscience and omnipotence. The theologians, for their part, have hardly responded to the opportunities open to them: it is still rare to find a theologian fully aware of the progress made in logic since the time of Kant. Until a rigorously formulated natural theology has been constructed, there seems to be little hope of commending theism at a serious level to a philosophical public. The construction of such a system will naturally be an enormous task, and the qualifications which it will require are formidable. Fortunately, it is not the purpose of this paper to put forward even prolegomena to such an enterprise.

Dogmatic Theology is not in the same position as Natural Theology. The dogmatic theologian does not have to wait for the natural theologian to be in a position to convince unbelieving philosophers of the existence and attributes of the one true God. It is already possible for him to apply the results of those philosophers' labours to assist him in his own thinking. Thirty years ago, such a thing was impossible, not so much because of the unbelief of philosophers as because of the irrelevance of their interests. Now the situation has changed. Philosophical discussion is not, in general, much more favourable to theism than it was, but it is greatly more relevant to it. Many examples could be given of contemporary philosophical discussions which are of immediate relevance to well-known problems of theology.

It seems to me important that theologians should be familiar with the work of their philosophical contemporaries on topics which fall within the interests of both. It is not, necessarily, that present-day philosophers are more acute or profound than their scholastic predecessors. It is rather that the modern theologian is unlikely really to get to grips with the thought of the classic scholastics unless he has been brought by the study of contemporary philosophy to a genuine appreciation of the problems in these fields. A man who cannot understand and evaluate the work of philosophers close to him in time and culture is unlikely to interpret without parody the difficult and remote thought of the scholastic doctors.

I do not intend to provide a list of recent discussions which have an interest for the theologian. Instead, I intend during the rest of this paper to show, with regard to a single topic, how much theologically relevant work is being done by philosophers working in the contemporary Anglo-American tradition. The topic I shall choose is transubstantiation, a subject which above all others seems at first glance medieval and remote from twentieth-century philosophical concern.

II

The doctrine of Transubstantiation is stated by the Council of Trent thus. In the sacrament of the Eucharist, when the bread and wine are consecrated the whole substance of the bread is thereby turned into the substance of the body of Christ our Lord and the whole substance of the wine is thereby turned into the substance of His blood. This turning of one substance into another, the Council affirmed, was aptly named by the holy Catholic Church: 'transubstantiation' (Session XIII, cap. 4).

This doctrine is expounded as follows in the twenty-fifth section of the second part of the Catechism of the Council of Trent. 'Now there are three wonderful and stupendous things which in this Sacrament, Holy Church without all doubt believes and confesses to be wrought by the words of consecration. The First is, That the true Body of Christ, that very same which was born of the Virgin, and now sits in Heaven at the Right-hand of the Father is contain'd in this Sacrament. The Second is that no substance of the Elements remains in it: Altho nothing seems more strange and distant to the senses. The Third, which is easily gather'd from both the former, tho the words of Consecration fully express it, is that what is beheld by the Eyes, or perceiv'd by the other Senses is in a wonderful and unspeakable manner, without any subject matter. And one may see indeed all the Accidents of Bread and Wine, which yet are inherent in no substance, but they consist of themselves; because the Substance of the Bread and Wine is so chang'd into the Body and Blood of the Lord, that the substance of the Bread and Wine altogether ceases.' (English edition of 1687, p. 208.)

In discussing this doctrine I wish altogether to abstract from the question, whether there is any good reason to believe it to be true. In particular, I wish to abstract from the question whether the exposition contained in the Tridentine Catechism is the only possible orthodox interpretation of the teaching of the Council. I wish to consider the purely philosophical question, whether the doctrine stated in that Catechism is or is not self-contradictory. If it is, then of course there can be no good reason to believe it true, no matter how august the authority which affirms it. On the other hand, if it does not appear self-contradictory, the question of its truth remains open for the philosopher. We cannot rule out from the start a philosophical position which accepted the coherence of the notion of transubstantiation, but rejected the possibility that it might be a doctrine revealed by God, on the grounds that a contradiction was to be found not in the notion of transubstantiation but in that of a divine revelation.

It might be thought that a philosopher could have no possibile interest in investigating the concept of transubstantiation unless he already believed it to be revealed by God. For the occurrence of transubstantiation, even if not logically impossible, is surely extremely improbable. But it is wrong to suppose that a philosopher should be interested in analysing descriptions only of states of affairs which are likely to obtain. Contemporary philosophers, like philosophers in all ages, frequently use the consideration of very improbable suppositions in order to throw light on concepts of great generality. Thus Strawson, in his book *Individuals* (London,

1959), devotes a whole chapter to the discussion of purely auditory experience such as would be enjoyed by beings who lacked all senses but that of hearing. Logicians talk of empty universes, and of the possibility of changing the past. In Wittgenstein's *Philosophical Investigations* we read of lions which talk, of dolls in pain, of disappearing chairs and languages of fantastic structure. The ability to imagine outlandish states of affairs is indeed a necessary skill for a philosopher. There is therefore no reason why the possibility of transubstantiation should not be investigated as a philosophical question in its own right, for the sake of the light such an inquiry might throw on concepts such as that of *material object*.

At the outset, it is obvious that if the true account of material objects is a phenomenalism such as that of Professor Ayer, then the notion of transubstantiation is self-contradictory. In his book *The Foundations of Empirical Knowledge* (London, 1940) Ayer wrote as follows in the chapter entitled 'The constitution of material things'. 'As for the belief in the "unity" and "substantiality" of material things, I shall show that it may be correctly represented as involving no more than the attribution to visual and tactual sense-data of certain relations which do, in fact, obtain in our experience.' On this view, to assert that a certain substance, e.g. bread, is or is not present in a certain place is to make a statement about what relations may be expected to obtain between sets of visual and tactual sense-data in our experience. But it is clear that a believer in transubstantiation who denies that the substance of bread is present on the altar after the consecration is not denying that all the relations between sense-data will obtain which would obtain if the substance, bread, really were present on the altar. As the Tridentine Catechism puts it: 'If the Faithful perswade themselves, that those things only are contain'd in this Sacrament, which are perceiv'd by the senses; they must needs be led into the greatest impiety, when with their Eyes, their Feeling, their Smell, their Taste, perceiving nothing at all, but the Species of Bread and Wine, they will judge that there is only Bread and Wine in the Sacrament.' If Ayer is right, therefore, the believer in transubstantiation is easily convicted of contradicting himself.

Since *The Foundations of Empirical Knowledge* was written, however, the doctrine which it contains has been severely criticized by people with no brief for transubstantiation, such as the late Professor J. L. Austin, whose posthumously published *Sense and Sensibilia* (Oxford, 1962) is almost entirely devoted to a refutation of Ayer's phenomenalism. Not all Austin's arguments are conclusive, but probably today most philosophers would agree with him in rejecting Ayer's claim that 'to say anything about a material thing is to say something, but not the same thing, about classes of sense-data' (cf. *Sense and Sensibilia*, p. 119).

If we reject phenomenalism, it might seem that we must say that behind the perceptible phenomena of any material object, there is an imperceptible part of it which is its substance. And indeed the Council of Trent, when it speaks of the substance of bread and wine, has frequently been taken – by believers and unbelievers alike – to have been speaking about a *part* of the bread and wine. The teaching of Trent is often expounded with the aid of a doctrine of substance which goes as follows. There are some parts of a loaf of bread, such as its shape and colour and taste, which can be perceived by the senses; but the substance which is beneath these outward parts is not perceptible to the senses. The perceptible parts or accidents of the bread may be pictured as concealing the inner reality which is the substance of the bread rather as a layer of paint may conceal the wood of a table. Whatever may be perceived of a material thing is only accidental to it: for each of the perceptible qualities of a thing may change and yet the thing remain the same. The substance of a thing is that in which these accidents inhere, the subject of which they are predicated. It is itself both imperceptible and indescribable: imperceptible, because all perceptible qualities are accidents; indescribable, because to describe a thing is to record its attributes, and attributes are what a substance has, not what it is.

I think it will be agreed that the doctrine of transubstantiation is often explained in this manner. Many who, like myself, find this account unacceptable, therefore reject transubstantiation. In fact it is very unlikely that the Council of Trent meant anything like the thesis we have just stated. It was not Trent, but Locke, who defined substance as some thing, we know not what, which supports the sensible qualities we find united in things. The account of substance accepted by the scholastics who worked out the theology of transubstantiation was not Locke's theory but the quite different one of Aristotle. The views of these scholastics are surely more relevant than those of Locke in determining what is likely to have been in the mind of the Fathers of Trent.

Commonly, in their Eucharistic theology, when these scholastics spoke of 'substance', they had in mind what Aristotle in his *Categories* called 'first substance'. The doctrine of the Categories has been stated in modern terms by Miss Anscombe in *Three Philosophers* (Oxford, 1961). '*First substance*,' she writes, 'is explained in the first place as what neither is asserted of nor exists in a subject: the examples offered are "such-and-such a man", "such-and-such a horse". A "first substance" then is what is designated by a proper name such as the name of a man or of a horse, or again, if one cared to give it a proper name, of a cabbage. A proper name is never, *qua* proper name, a predicate. Thus what a proper name stands for is not *asserted of* a subject.' A surface, such as the surface of a particular wedding-ring, is not *asserted of* a subject, but in Aristotle's sense it is *in* a subject. First substance, therefore, is described by contrast with what is *asserted of* and what *exists in* a subject (*Three Philosophers*, pp. 7–8).

In the *Categories*, Aristotle lists ten different types of predication. A predicate may tell you what kind of thing something is, or how big it is, or what it is like, or where it is, or what it is doing, and so on. We may say, for instance, of Christ that he was a man, that he was six feet tall, that he was a good man, that he was younger than John the Baptist, that he lived in Galilee, that he lived under Pontius Pilate, that he sat upon Jacob's well, that he wore a beard, that he healed the sick, and that he was crucified. The predicates which we use in saying these things belong to different categories: they belong, respectively, to the categories of substance, quantity, quality, relation, place, time, posture, *habitus*, *actio* and *passio*.

'Substance' is here clearly being used in a sense different from that in which it occurs in the phrase 'first substance'. Geach, following Aquinas, has recently drawn a distinction between substantival and adjectival terms. 'Aquinas calls our attention,' he writes, 'to a feature of Latin grammar – that substantives are singular or plural on their own account, whereas adjectives "agree in number" with substantives (*Summa Theologiae Ia*, 39, 3c and *ad*

1; 5 *ad* 5). This suggests to him a logical distinction between two sorts of terms: substantival terms, to which the question "how many?" applies directly, and adjectival terms, to which this question applies only in so far as they are used to add a qualification to substantival terms. One may ask how many cats there are in a room; but not, how many black things there are in the room; only, how many black *cats* (say) there are in the room. The basis of this distinction is that the sense of "cat" determines a sense for "one and the same cat", whereas the sense of "black thing" does not in the least determine what shall count as one and the same black thing.' (*Three Philosophers*, p. 86; *Reference and Generality*, pp. 39–40.)

Geach's distinction take us only part of the way to understanding Aristotle's distinction between predicates in the category of substance and predicates in the other nine, accidental, categories. A substantival term is not the same as a substantial term. 'Gold' is a predicate in the category of substance; yet we cannot ask 'how many golds are there in the room?'. On the other hand, the noun 'city' determines a sense for 'one and the same city', yet 'city' does not stand for a kind of substance.

The notion of a substantial predicate, as Miss Anscombe has insisted, is closely connected with a particular sense of the question 'What is that?' which might be asked while pointing to something. 'We can pick out that sense of "What is it?" that is answered by the name of a kind of thing or of a kind of stuff: "That is sulphur", "That is an oak-tree", "That is a hyena".' ' "Substance",' writes Miss Anscombe, 'is a classification, but whether of things or of concepts (or words) seems difficult to determine. If we ask what falls into the category of substances the answer is "e.g. men, horses, cabbages, gold, sugar, soap". This answer mentions things, not concepts or words, so substance might seem to be a classification of things.' On the other hand, we cannot ask: in virtue of what characteristics are these things all substances. For a description of their characteristics would already be a description in the form: description of the properties of substances. It is not just a well-established hypothesis that gold or a cat is a substance: that e.g. the question 'What is it made of?' has an application to a cat or a lump of gold. (*Three Philosophers*, p. 13.)

Aristotle devoted much thought to the relationship between first substance and predicates in the category of substance. Consider a sentence which contains a predication in the category of substance, such as 'Socrates is a man'. The name 'Socrates' stands for the individual, or first substance, Socrates. Now what does the predicate '. . . [is] a man' stand for? A Platonist might say that it stands for humanity as such. But this answer is not open to an Aristotelian: he rejects the idea that there is such a thing as humanity as such. The answer which Aristotle gives to this question is that the predicate stands for exactly the same thing as the subject does; that is to say, it stands for, or refers to, Socrates himself.

On the other hand, in a sentence containing a predication in one of the other categories, such as 'Socrates is white', the subject and the predicate do not stand for the same thing. The subject, 'Socrates' stands for the man Socrates; but the predicate '. . . [is] white' does not stand for Socrates. Does it stand for whiteness? Only a Platonist could say this. The answer given in the Aristotelian tradition was that it stood for the 'individualized form', the whiteness of Socrates.[1]

Such was the interpretation given by scholastics of the doctrines of Aristotle in Metaphysics Λ and Z. If we seek a definition of 'substance' and 'accidents' in this tradition, we must say that the substance of a thing is what a predicate in the category of substance, which is true of that thing, stands for; and the accidents of a thing are what true predicates of it in the other nine categories stand for. Thus, if it is true that Peter is a man, then the substance of Peter is what the predicate '. . . [is] a man' stands for, to wit, Peter himself; and if it is true that Peter is clever, then among the

---

1 A modern philosopher would speak naturally of the predicate of 'Socrates is a man' as being '. . . is a man'. Aquinas, though in his commentary on the *De Interpretatione* he recognizes the use now common, usually spoke of a predicate as a single term like 'man'. In a sentence such as 'Socrates is a man', if 'Socrates' and 'man' both stand for Socrates, what, if anything, does 'is' stand for? Aquinas's answer was that 'is' stood for *esse* – an *esse* which differed systematically accordingly as the predicate following the 'is' differed in category. (*In V. Met*, Cathala 890.)

accidents of Peter will be whatever the predicate '. . . is clever' stands for in the sentence 'Peter is clever'.

Now most modern philosophers would object to saying that predicates of any kind, whether substantial or accidental, *stand for* anything at all. Names stand for, or refer to, what they name; but there is nothing which '. . . is a man' or '. . . is clever' stands for in the way in which 'Peter' stands for Peter. To be sure, '. . . is a man' and '. . . is clever' have meaning. But so do 'if' and 'but' have meaning; they are not empty noises. But no one supposes that they stand for some ifhood and butness existing in the world. So many philosophers would argue: a typical example is Quine in his essay 'On what there is' (*From a Logical Point of View* Cambridge, Mass., 1953).[2]

I am inclined to accept their argument, for the following reason. It seems clear that all the words in a sentence must stand for the same thing whether the sentence is true or false. If a question admits of the answer 'Yes' or 'No', the reference of all the words in the question must be the same no matter what the answer may be. But if the sentence 'Peter is clever' is false, there is no such thing as the cleverness of Peter for the sentence to be about. Therefore, the sentence 'Peter is clever', whether true or false, cannot contain any phrase or word which refers to the cleverness of Peter.[3]

For this reason I find it difficult to accept that accidents are the references of accidental predicates. But although many of the scholastics accepted such a theory, it does not seem necessary to do so in order to make sense of the teaching of Trent. All that it is necessary to believe is that the wisdom of Socrates, say, exists if and only if Socrates is wise. It is not necessary to believe, as these

---

2 On the other hand, there *are* modern philosophers who are prepared to accept the idea that predicates have references. Strawson, (*Individuals*, p. 144), considers whether in 'Raleigh smokes' the expression 'smokes' can be said to stand for smoking, or the habit of smoking. He says: 'I know of no rule or custom which makes it always senseless or incorrect to say this, any more than I know of any rule or custom which would make it always senseless or incorrect to say that an assertion made in the words "Raleigh smokes" was an assertion about smoking.'

3 The form of this argument goes back to Buridan (Geach, *Reference and Generality*, p. xi).

scholastics did, that this wisdom is actually referred to in the sentence 'Socrates is wise'. It is not difficult to find modern philosophers who are prepared to subscribe to the much more modest thesis that if Socrates is wise then there is such a thing as the wisdom of Socrates, and if Socrates is not wise then there is no such thing as the wisdom of Socrates.

Mr Strawson, for instance, in his widely acclaimed book *Individuals*, discusses ways in which particular and universal terms may be tied to each other. We may distinguish, say, particular utterances, and particular catches at cricket. We can then group together some particular utterances as wise utterances, and some particular catches as difficult catches. We are in that case grouping particulars by means of universals which are attached or 'tied' to them. But we may also group particulars by tying them to other particulars: as we may group together Socrates's utterances, and Carr's catches. In cases where we have two particulars tied together in this way, we often find that one particular will be an independent member of the tie, and the other particular a dependent member. For instance, Socrates may be tied to many particular utterances, but any particular utterance of his cannot be tied to any other particular person. Particulars, such as Socrates, which are the independent members of all such ties as they enter into, are called by Strawson: 'independent particulars'. As he explicitly recognizes, Strawson's notion of *independent particular* is very close to Aristotle's notion of *first substance*.[4]

To an Aristotelian, the natural meaning of the decree of Trent which states that the substance of bread and wine turns into the substance of Christ's body and blood, is not that some part of the bread and wine turns into some part of the body and blood, but simply that the bread and wine turns into the body and blood. Following Aquinas (in *1 Cor 11:24*), the Fathers of Trent used 'the substance of Christ's body' and 'Christ's body' as interchangeable terms. According to scholastic theory, substance is not an imperceptible part of a particular individual. It is not a part of an individual; it *is* that individual. And it is imperceptible by the senses only in the following sense: I do not see *what kind of a thing*

4 *Individuals*, pp. 167–70.

something is with my eyes as I see *what colour* it is with my eyes, any more than I see *what it tastes like* with my eyes. For all that, substances may be perceived. I can see, say, sulphuric acid with my eyes; though it is not just by looking, but by intelligent use of hypothesis and experiment and information, that I know that the stuff I see is sulphuric acid. Similarly, when I see sugar, what I see is sweet, though it is not with my eyes that I discover this. *A pari*, before the consecration the substance of bread is *not* imperceptible: what I see is bread; the substance which I see is the substance, bread.

Transubstantiation is a *unique* conversion, a turning of one thing into another which has no parallel. In all other cases where A turns into B there is some stuff which is first A-ish, and then B-ish. As scholastics would say, the same matter is first informed with the form of A-ishness and then informed with the form of B-ishness. (This sentence is merely a restatement, not an explanation, of the sentence which precedes it.) But in the Eucharistic *conversio* there is no parcel of stuff which is first bread and then Chirst's body; not only does one form give way to another but one bit of matter gives way to another. In an ordinary change, when the form of A-ishness gives way to the form of B-ishness, we have a trans*formation* – substantial transformation, or accidental transformation, according to whether the forms in question are substantial forms or accidental forms, that is to say, according to whether the predicates '. . . is an A' and '. . . is a B' are accidental or substantial predicates. In the Eucharist we have not just one form giving way to another, but one substance giving way to another: not just transformation, but trans*substant*iation.

It may well be asked at this point: what is now left of the notion of *turning into* here? To my knowledge, no completely satisfactory answer to this question has yet been given; nor do I think that I can succeed where others have failed. But it may help if we explain how the notion of *turning into* came to have a place in discussion of the Eucharist at all. There is no mention in Scriptural references to this sacrament of anything turning into anything else: why is there in Trent?

Aquinas introduces the notion of *turning into* as the only possible explanation of the presence of Christ's body under the appearances of bread and wine after the consecration. After the consecration it is true to say that Christ is in such-and-such a place. Now there are only three ways, says Aquinas, in which something can begin to exist in a place in which it did not exist before. Either it moves to that place from another place; or it is created in that place; or something which is already in that place turns, or is turned, into it. But Christ's body does not move into the place where the Eucharistic species are, nor is it created, since it already exists. Therefore something – to wit, the bread and wine – is turned into it.

It is essential to St Thomas's account that the bread and wine should cease to be, not by being annihilated, but by being *turned into* the body and blood. Transubstantiation is sometimes explained thus: the bread and wine are annihilated, and in their place Christ's body begins to exist. But for St Thomas there could be no sense in saying that Christ's body existed *in such-and-such a place* if the bread and wine formerly existing in that place had been annihilated. For, he would ask, how is the connection made between the body on the right hand of the Father and this particular altar? The connection, for him, is this, and only this: that the accidents of what has been turned into Christ's body are in such-and-such a place. Take away the transubstantiation, according to St Thomas, and you take away the presence.

The accidents which remain, says the Tridentine Catechism, following the Council of Constance, remain without a subject. Believers in transubstantiation are sometimes wrongly thought to hold that the accidents after consecration inhere in the substance of Christ's body.[5] If this were so then, for example, the whiteness which the bread once had would become the whiteness of Christ. And thus all the accidental predicates which are true of the sacramental host would become true of Christ: it would be true that Christ was white and round and two inches across and smaller than an orange.

When we consider the concept of accidents inherent in no substance, examples come to mind which are either incredible or too straightforward. The idea of the Cheshire cat's grin without the cat seems the very quintessence of absurdity. On the other hand

5 Cf. Hobbes, *Leviathan*, I, viii (Everyman edition, p. 40).

there is nothing miraculous or mysterious in there being a smell of onions after the onions have ceased to exist. The smell of onions is just the sort of thing which St Thomas meant by an accident in this context. When he discusses the question how accidents without substance can nourish and inebriate he considers the suggestion that it is the smell of wine which inebriates, as the smell of wine in a full cellar may make you feel dizzy before you broach a cask. He rejects this suggestion, not on the grounds that an accident is a different sort of thing altogether, but on the grounds that you can get far more drunk on consecrated wine than you can by going into a cellar and sniffing. But perhaps a better example of an accident without a substance than any known to St Thomas is the colour of the sky. When the sky is blue, its blueness is not the blue *of* any substance. 'The sky' is the name not of a substance, but of a phenomenal object (like 'the host') and there is no substance *in* the sky which is blue.

The principle that the accidents of the host do not inhere in the substance of Christ's body is one which is often violated in popular preaching of the Eucharist. '. . . is moved', '. . . is dropped', '. . . is spat upon' are accidental predicates. Consequently, if the host is moved, Christ is not moved; if the host is dropped, Christ is not dropped; if the host is spat upon, Christ is not spat upon. In the words of Cardinal Newman: 'Our Lord neither descends from heaven upon our altars nor moves when carried in procession. The visible species change their position but he does not move (*Via Media*, 1877, ii. 220).' The principle to which Newman alludes is violated in popular devotions to 'The Prisoner of the Tabernacle'; it was violated also by Cardinal Pole when he forced an unfortunate heretic to repeat the words of the recanting Berengar: 'The real body and blood of our Lord Jesus Christ . . . are held and broken by the hands of the priests and are crushed by the teeth of the faithful.'[6]

The principle that the accidents inhere in no substance, however, leaves one problem with which I shall conclude. Among the accidental categories of Aristotle is the category of place. '. . . is on

6 I am indebted for these last two references to the Rev. H. Green, C. R.

the altar', for instance, is an accidental predicate. But if the accidents which once belonged to the bread do not inhere after consecration in the substance of Christ's body, then it appears that it by no means follows from the presence of the host upon the altar that Christ is present on the altar. Thus the doctrine of transubstantiation appears in the end to fail to secure that for which alone it was originally introduced, namely the real presence of Christ's body under the sacramental species. I do not know of any satisfactory answer to this problem. If I did, I would give it. Since I do not, I must leave it, as the writers of textbooks say, as an exercise for the reader.

2

The Development of Ecclesiastical Doctrine

The development of doctrine is not itself a doctrine of the Catholic Church. From the beginning, the Church has taught, not that its dogmas develop, but that its faith is immutable. St Paul told the Galatians: 'Even if we, or an angel from heaven, should preach to you a gospel contrary to that which we preach to you, let him be accursed. As we have said before, so now I say again, if anyone is preaching to you a gospel contrary to that which you received, let him be accursed' (Galatians, 1, 8). Quoting those words 400 years later, Pope Simplicius wrote 'one and the same norm of apostolic doctrine continues in the apostles' successors'. The Council of Trent, in its preamble, asserted that the Gospel truth is to be found in the written books, and unwritten traditions, which were received by the Apostles from the mouth of Christ, or dictated to them by the Holy Spirit; which have been handed down to us and preserved by continuous succession in the Catholic Church. Pius IX, writing against Günther in 1857, spoke of the 'perennial immutability of the faith' which he contrasted with 'philosophy and human sciences which are neither self-consistent nor free from errors of many kinds'. The Syllabus of 1864 condemned the view that divine revelation was imperfect and might progress in step with the progress of human reason. The Vatican Council repeated this. 'The doctrine of faith which God has revealed is not, like a philosophical theory, something for human ingenuity to perfect; but rather divine deposit from Christ to his bride, to be faithfully preserved and infallibly explained.' The immutability of dogma is not a matter of words only but of meaning also: 'That sense is always to be given to sacred dogmas which holy mother Church has once explained; it is never to be given up under the pretext of a more profound understanding.'[1]

The only mention of the development of doctrine in official ecclesiastical documents occurs in the unflattering context of the modernist crisis. The encyclical *Lamentabili* attributes to the modernists the following view: 'The objects of religious sensibility, since it is coextensive with the Absolute, has infinitely many aspects, of which one may be clear at one moment, and another at the next. In a similar manner, the condition of believers is not always and everywhere the same. It follows that the formulae which we call dogmas must be subject to the same vicissitudes, and therefore must be capable of alteration. Thus there is nothing to prevent an intrinsic evolution of doctrine.' Such a view was described by Pius X as an unending tissue of sophistries, which wrecks and ruins all religion.

Many of the condemned modernist propositions were concerned with the development of doctrine. Two of the most interesting read as follows. (1) The revelation which constitutes the object of Catholic belief was not completed with the Apostles. (2) The principal articles of the Apostles' Creed did not have the same meaning for the early Christians as they have for Christians of the present day.[2]

Against this array of pronouncements hostile to the notion of development two passages must be set. The first is a text of Vincent of Lerins quoted at the Vatican: 'May the understanding, knowledge, and wisdom of all and each, of the individual and of the Church, grow and progress mightily as the years and ages pass, but always in the same doctrine, in the same sense, and in the same belief.' The second is a letter of Pius X written in 1908 which said that the condemnations of modernism were not directed against the views of Cardinal Newman who was and remains the most

---

1 See H. Denzinger and C. Bannwart, *Enchiridon Symbolorum*, 25 edn, pp. 783, 1795, 1800, 1817.

2 Ibid., 2021, 2060ff.

distinguished Catholic exponent of the notion of doctrinal development.[3]

It is clear from the texts which I have cited that when we speak of the development of doctrine we are not referring to some doctrine, or meta-doctrine, of the Church concerning its own teaching. Rather we are alluding to a theory, or set of theories, to account for certain general and obvious facts about the Church's doctrine; and in particular to reconcile the course of the Church's history with the dogma of the immutability of faith. To deny flatly that dogma develops would not necessarily be heretical; it would merely argue great ignorance of history.

It is first of all obvious that the number of defined dogmas has grown constantly since the earliest Councils. Beliefs whose acceptance is now a condition of membership of the Church were formerly rejected by men who retained the communion and favour of the Apostolic See. It is well known that St Clement of Alexandria held views upon the Eucharist, and St John Chrysostom upon Predestination, and St Thomas Aquinas on the Immaculate Conception, which, if expressed in 1870, would have made it impossible for any of them to take part in the deliberations of the Vatican Council. At that Council there was defined a doctrine whose definitions many of the attending Bishops opposed until the last moment; and in our own day Pope Pius XII proclaimed, for the first time under the sanction of an anathema, the doctrine of the assumption of Mary.

The multiplication of definitions does not, merely in itself, raise any problem concerning the immutability of faith. The avowed purpose of the majority of conciliar and papal definitions has not been to make change or addition to the beliefs of orthodox Christians, but rather to provide a legal instrument for the reform or expulsion of heretics alleged to have denied an article of faith hitherto an unquestioned part of the Christian patrimony of belief. It has never, so far as I know, been officially defined that Jesus was a man – a male, and not a woman – because there has never been a feminist heresy to deny this truth. But if a group began to propound

3 *Acta Apostolicae Sedis*, 1, 200f.

such a heresy, and it was condemned under anathema, the Pope could scarcely be reproached with altering, or adding to, the faith handed down from the Apostles.

It is impossible, however, to produce an actual case of a definition on any major topic which can be seen beyond all possibility of cavil to be merely a reaffirmation of a belief held unanimously by Christians until the appearance of the heresy which provoked the anathema. Theologians sometimes quote with approval the dictum of St Vicent of Lerins, that the object of faith is what has been believed at all times and in all places by all Christians: *quod semper, quod ubique, quod ab omnibus*. Taken seriously, this dictum would rule out all articles of faith except those contained in the Apostle's Creed, and perhaps some of those. There is an ambiguity, of course, in the phrase 'ab omnibus'. Does this mean 'by all who have claimed to be Christians'? If so, then the dictum is patently false of the corpus of doctrine which is now imposed under pain of excommunication. Does it mean 'by all orthodox Christians'? Here again, we must distinguish. If 'orthodox Christians' means 'orthodox by the defined standards of the time in which they lived' then again the dictum is false. If it means 'orthodox by the defined standards of the present day' then it is true; but trivially so, and only at the cost of making heretics of a large number of Fathers, Saints, and Doctors of the Church. For there has been scarcely any major definition of Pope or Council which has not contradicted the recorded views of one or other of the bishops and theologians of the early centuries of the Church.

To illustrate the difficulties against the doctrine of the immutability of dogma, I shall mention four dogmas of the Christian faith, each defined under anathema at different periods of history: the dogma of the Blessed Trinity, the teaching concerning the particular judgement and the beatific vision before the resurrection, the prohibition of usury, and the definition of the Assumption of Mary into Heaven.

The dogma of the Trinity was defined early in the history of the Church, and its expression has remained stable for many centuries. On such a cardinal doctrine, if anywhere, one would expect to find a unanimous testimony from the beginning to the faith which we now recognize as orthodox. But it is not so. Let me quote Newman on the difficulty of securing a consensus of ante-Nicene divines to the doctrine defined at Nicea and later councils,

> The Catholic truth in question is made up of a number of separate propositions, each of which, if maintained to the exclusion of the rest, is a heresy. In order then to prove that all the ante-Nicene writers taught the dogma of the Holy Trinity, it is not enough to prove that each has gone far enough to be a heretic – not enough to prove that one has held that the Son is God (for so did the Sabellian, so did the Macedonian), and another that the Father is not the Son (for so did the Arian) and another that the Son is equal to the father (for so did the Tritheist), and another that there is but One God (for so did the Unitarian) . . . but we must show that all these statements at once, and others too, are laid down by as many separate testimonies as many fairly be taken to constitute a consensus of doctors.

Newman went on to summarize the evidence. The Creeds of the period make no mention in their letter of the Catholic doctrine. The only great Council of ante-Nicene times condemned, or at least withdrew, the use of the word 'homoousion' to express the relation of the Son to the Father: the word which, after Nicea, was the criterion of orthodoxy. He writes:

> The six great bishops and Saints of the antenicene Church were St Irenaeus, St Hippolytus, St Cyprian, St Gregory Thaumaturgus, St Dionysius of Alexandria and St Methodius. Of these St Dionysius is accused by St Basil of having sown the first seeds of Arianism; and St Gregory is allowed by the same learned father to have used language concerning our Lord, which he only defends on the plea of an economical object in the writer. St Hippolytus speaks as if he were ignorant of our Lord's eternal Sonship, St Methodius speaks incorrectly at least upon the Incarnation; and St Cyprian does not treat of theology at all. Such is the incompleteness of the extant teaching of these true saints, and, in their day, faithful witnesses of the eternal Son.[4]

4 The two passages quoted are from *The Development of Doctrine* (London, 1960, pp. 11–12).

Newman's purpose in writing thus was neither to propose difficulties against the doctrine of the immutability of faith nor to impugn the orthodoxy of the fathers of the first centuries. Rather he wished to suggest to his fellow-Anglicans that if they accepted the Nicene formulae in face of such incomplete evidence in their favour from the primitive Church, they had no reason for rejecting the primacy of the Roman See about which, he claimed, the surviving records were considerably more eloquent. None the less, the case which he presents raises an obvious problem for the doctrine which we are considering; a problem which scholarship since Newman's day has done little to mitigate and something to aggravate.

A millenium after Nicea, Pope Benedict XII defined as a truth of faith that the souls of the faithful departed, once they have been purified from sin if necessary, are taken to heaven and there enjoy, before the resurrection of their bodies, the beatific vision of God. The circumstances which led to the definition of this now so familiar doctrine are well known. Pope Benedict's predecessor John XXII had preached, and had retracted only on his deathbed, the doctrine that the Saints would begin to enjoy the vision of God only after the resurrection and the general judgement. They were meanwhile, he had maintained, in a state of imperfect happiness, blessed with the company of Christ's human nature, but not yet in the joy of the Lord.

These circumstances are well known. What is perhaps less well known, is that the view put forward by John XXII seems, on the evidence we have, to have been the common one before the time of the great scholastics. The New Testament has little to say about the fate of the soul between death and the return of Christ: what little it says – e.g. St Paul's wish to 'be away from the body and at home with the Lord' – is as compatible with the heresy of Pope John as with the orthodoxy of Pope Benedict. The prayer of the Mass that the faithful departed may be received into a place of rest and light and peace, seems a rather cool and unenthusiastic description for the beatific vision. A letter of St Ambrose is a good example of the eschatological picture current in his time. The apostles and the martyrs, he thought, already enjoyed the beatific vision; but the rest of men had not yet entered into their everlasting destiny. Their souls were housed in spiritual warehouses, sorted but not yet despatched, in three groups. The wicked were being punished, but not yet in Hell; run-of-the-mill sinners were to be tried by fire after the last judgement; the just enjoy a certain rest, but suffer still as they wait for the number of the elect to be filled up. Similar views, though not so quaintly explicit, are to be found in St Augustine and St Gregory. As late as the twelfth century St Bernard preached that the faithful departed, though 'at their ease, being freed from the confining flesh' still 'await a perfection which will come only from the resurrection of the body' and are not yet 'with the angels' nor enjoying 'the satisfaction of glory'. It was to St Bernard that Pope John XXII appealed in his ill-starred sermon at Avignon.[5]

The condemnation as heretical of the opinion that usury is not a sin took place in the lifetime of Pope John XXII. Here the case is reversed: it is not the prehistory of a defined doctrine which presents a difficulty but rather the subsequent attitude of official Catholicism. For centuries before and after the Council of Vienne it was taught, with every possible emphasis, that it was a sin to charge interest on money lent. The condemnation of usury in the Middle Ages were more formal and more grievously sanctioned than any condemnation of artificial contraception in our own day. No-one could say that detestation of usury was nowadays a notable mark of a church whose bishops impose on their clergy an obligation of fruitful investment of ecclesiastical moneys and who are sometimes inclined to see the capitalist societies of the West as Godsent champions of the right against the evils of Communism. This change is comparatively recent. As late as 1745 it was taught, in the encyclical *Vix Pervenit*, that it was a sin to ask for more money back than one had lent; any money however little, demanded over and above the return of the principal, was illicitly acquired. The encyclical admitted that there might be legitimate grounds other than that of the loan itself on which a consideration might be demanded beyond the principal; but it concluded: 'It must be carefully noted that anyone who says that there are *always* such

---

5 St Ambrose, Ep. 35, 7 (J. P. Migne, *Patrologiae Cursus Completus, series latiba*, henceforth. P. L., pp. 16, 1125); St Bernard, Sermons (P. L., pp. 183, 325, 528, 698). See H. Rondet, S. J., *Do Dogmas Change?* (London, 1962), pp. 22–35.

grounds attached to a loan would be rashly persuading himself of falsehood.' Compare this with the brief statement of an approved modern manual of moral theology. 'The lender may not, as a rule, require a remuneration for the thing lent. For extrinsic reasons, however, which nowadays are always verified, in case money is lent, a just rate of interest may be charged.'

Consider finally the dogma of the Assumption. Pope Pius XII declared in 1950 that it was dogma divinely revealed, and to be believed under pain of anathema, that the Blessed Virgin Mary at the end of her earthly life, was raised body and soul to heavenly glory. His predecessor, Pius X, had declared that the revelation which constituted the object of Christian faith was complete with last Apostle. It follows that the doctrine of the Assumption must have been revealed before the death of the last Apostle. Yet the records which we have show no trace of a belief in the Assumption before the end of the fourth century; a gap as wide as that which separates us from Queen Elizabeth's death. The first references to the belief occur either in spurious and legendary treatises or in hesitant passages in genuine sermons. Only with the liturgical establishment of the feast of the Dormition on 15 August (*c.* 650) have we, in the collect and office of the day, a clear witness to the doctrine. There could hardly be a clearer example of the difficulties attendant on the doctrine of the immutability of the faith and of the nature of the phenomena to be explained by any theory of the development of doctrine.

Various explanations have been offered by Catholics of these problematic cases. Sometimes, we are told, doctrines held implicitly are only later explicitly formulated. Other dogmas are deductions from the reading of Scripture. Some variations between ancient and modern teaching may be due to a degree of corruption. Many doctrines may have been believed for centuries without leaving any written record. I will examine how far these explanations can account for the phenomena of development.

1. *Formulation.* It is often said that we believe the same as the first Christians, only they believed implicitly what we believed explicitly. In support of this theory reference is sometimes made to S.T. IIa, IIae 1, 7 where St Thomas asserts that whatever more recent people

have believed was contained in the faith of the fathers who proceeded them, but implicitly. St Thomas, however, was considering the relation not between the faith of later and earlier Christians, but between the faith of Christians and the Hebrew patriarchs. Since revelation continued between the age of the patriarchs and the time of the Apostles, it will not suffice to say that modern Catholics have the same faith as St Peter in the same sense in which St Peter had the same faith as Abraham. Even for the purpose which he had in mind, St Thomas's use of 'implicitly' seems very strained. He says that belief e.g. in the Virgin Birth is contained implicitly in belief in God's providence. To clarify this he compares it to the way in which all other principles are contained in the principle of contradiction. It is difficult to make any credible sense of this Aristotelian dictum which is at all helpful in connection with the development of dogma.

The notion of implicit belief is, of course, a valid one, and has many applications in the history of dogma. If it is the case that being a perfect human being involves possessing adrenal glands, then it is quite natural to say that the fathers of Chalcedon believed implicitly that Christ possessed adrenal glands. But it is a different matter to say that St Irenaeus believed implicitly in the Immaculate Conception because he compared our Lady to Eve, or to say that ante-Nicene writers, whose words explicitly contradict the teaching of the Council, implicitly believed in Nicene orthodoxy.

2. *Deduction.* There are certainly some dogmas which are, and are put forward as, deductions from other dogmas or from Scripture; as the doctrine that Christ had two wills follows from the doctrine that he had two natures. But the relation of some dogmas to the Scriptures seems not to be that of conclusion to premisses, but rather that of hypothesis to data: I mean that a dogma such as the Nicene and Constantinopolitan formulation of the Trinity seems to supply a set of premisses from which the Scriptural statements about the Father, Son and Holy Ghost may be derived as conclusions, rather than a set of conclusions which may be derived from the words of Scripture as premisses. This pattern seems to apply particularly to those now defined dogmas each of which is first recorded as one among a number of competing theological

theories to account for the data of revelation; I am thinking particularly of the definitions concerning justification, from Orange to the Synod of Pistoia. It is certain that heresies are condemned normally not because they do not follow from Scripture, nor even because they contradict something which follows from Scripture, but rather because from them there follows something which contradicts Scripture.

But there are some doctrines, such as the Immaculate Conception and the Assumption, which do not seem to be in a deductive relationship to scripture any more than does the canonization of a particular Saint. The difficulty here has led some writers on development to dangerous sophistry; saying that the development of doctrine 'occurs in conformity with a logic which is rigorous and unescapable' but that 'the process by which a truth of the faith is derived from one that precedes it takes place wholly in the night of faith' according to a 'logic of God' which is 'above ours' and which 'goes beyond the purely rational expression which we instinctively try to give it'.

3. *Corruption.* Since the Reformation, it has been a commonplace outside the Roman communion to account for the variations between Catholic teaching at different periods by regarding recently defined doctrines as Romish corruptions. Such a course is naturally not open to a Catholic; but Catholics concede that the charism of infallibility guarantees only that the Church's official magisterium will not teach anything which it ought not to teach; not that it will teach everything which it ought to teach at any given period of its history. A further question can be raised concerning the limits of infallibility. Is it possible that a Pope might be mistaken in thinking that he was speaking ex-cathedra? The charism extends only to matters concerning faith and morals. Would it be possible for a Pope to believe mistakenly that a certain belief was necessary to salvation, and therefore within his competence to define? If not, then is there no criterion of what pertains to the deposit of faith independent of what Popes have said, or may say, in their definitions? If so, then how is it known that – e.g. in defining the Assumption – the Pope did not perhaps go beyond his competence and was therefore deprived of the

charism of infallibility and perhaps erred?

4. *Unrecorded belief.* The decree of the Council of Trent quoted earlier is quite naturally read as implying that the Gospel truth is contained partly in the written records which make up Scripture and partly in unrecorded beliefs which have been orally transmitted from generation to generation. Theologians, faced with the task of accounting for the emergence of an apparently new doctrine, have sometimes solved their difficulties by claiming that the doctrine had always been explicitly believed since the time of the Apostles, but that no record of such a belief had survived. The absence of records in such cases is sometimes shrugged off as the result of chance, sometimes accounted for by appeal to a *disciplina arcani* or deliberate concealment of esoteric doctrines by the early Christians.

Now there is nothing inconceivable in the faithful transmission, over long periods, of a piece of oral tradition. In the nature of the case, one cannot produce a conclusive proof of its possibility by pointing to the present existence of an accurate record of a remote event which has been transmitted *purely* orally. But there are many pieces of lore which, though they may be found in print at various times, are almost always acquired by hearing and passed on by word of mouth. Examples are nursery rhymes, bawdy songs and jokes, the way to tie complicated knots, and simple and staple prayers. Monsignor Knox has pointed out that the Lord's Prayer has been transmitted from the time of the Apostles almost entirely by word of mouth: most of those who have known it have been illiterate and almost all of us learnt it at an age when we were too young to read. The unimportance of written, as compared with oral, influence here may be gauged by the surprise with which Catholics make the discovery – if they ever do – that the Doway version reads 'Our Father which art in heaven . . .'. Iona and Peter Opie, in *The Lore and Language of School Children* (Oxford, 1959), give some striking examples of the transmission from child to child, over centuries, of beliefs which though recorded in books were not written in any place where a child would be likely to read them. Such are the beliefs that a cut between thumb and forefinger causes lockjaw, that dock-leaves cure nettle stings (mentioned by Chaucer), that finding a four-leaved clover brings luck (recorded in

1620) and that stepping on two flagstones at once brings disaster (a belief which Dr Johnson never grew out of). (Ibid. pp. 1, 62, 221, 223.)

If the existence of an oral tradition independent of the Scriptures is not inconceivable, it is not, on the other hand, an item of Catholic faith. For the fathers and the great Scholastics all the truths which are necessary to salvation are contained in the Scriptures; 'tradition' means the handing on and interpreting of the Scriptures, not a set of beliefs side by side with them. The suggestion that there are some Catholic truths which have been derived from the Apostles by oral transmission was first made, it seems, by Ockham. This view was taken up by fifteenth-century theologians, and became naturally popular with anti-Lutheran polemists. It was the view held by the majority of the fathers present at the Council of Trent, but it was not defined by the Council, as has recently been brilliantly shown by George Tavard. The original draft of the decree on tradition, championed by the Papal Legate, and using language derived, oddly enough, from King Henry VIII, spoke of the Gospel truth as being 'contained partly in written books, partly in unwritten traditions'. A vociferous minority, including the Bishop of Worcester and Cardinal Pole, opposed the draft. Typical of their attitude was the statement of Angelo Bonuti, the general of the Servites, 'I consider that all evangelical truth is in Scripture, not therefore *partly*'. To secure unanimity, the words 'partim . . . partim . . . ' were dropped from the final decree, which thus deliberately left room for the classical, but by then unpopular, conception of tradition as an interpreter of, rather than a supplement to, Scripture.[6]

It is obvious, and we are told expressly by the Gospel writers, that while men lived who remembered Jesus, there were many facts about his life and teaching which were known but which were never committed to writing. It does not follow from this, however, that any of these facts were still known and repeated some generations later, after the formation and circulation of the canonical scriptures. That by the fifth century there were still current reliable oral traditions of this kind seems unlikely for the following reasons.

6 *Holy Writ or Holy Church*, (London, 1963), ch. 12.

It is rare today to find stories circulating concerning persons who lived or events which happened much more than 100 years ago which can plausibly claim both to be reliable and to have been transmitted only by word of mouth. The examples of oral tradition mentioned earlier all concern frequently repeated formulae, or are connected with often repeated actions. Fidelity of transmission is much more credible in such contexts than in the case of a narrative of a particular event which there is not frequent reason to repeat or of a statement of abstruse theory.

Since the institution of the feast of 15 August, and especially since the rosary became popular, the doctrine of the Assumption has belonged precisely to that class of beliefs whose oral propagation is most credible: even today, probably far more Catholics first heard of the Assumption in connection with the holiday of obligation or of learning to tell their beads rather than through the reading of pious books or catechisms. But this does not yet make it credible that the belief was transmitted orally from the time of the death of St Mary until the period at which it is first recorded.

It may be argued that the parallel with the present day does not hold; first because we live in a much more literate age, and secondly because we do not know that there were not written records of the belief, say from the second century, which have been lost. This is so: but there are particular as well as general reasons for doubting the survival of oral tradition concerning evangelical events after the second century. Christian writers in the third and later centuries never make appeal to such traditions, other than liturgical ones, and write as if the canonical scriptures contained all the information which had survived about the life of our Lord and his circle. Origen, for example, writing about the authorship of the Epistle to the Hebrews, cannot appeal to any reliable tradition on this point: he bases his guess about the Epistle's composition on its style and content. The manifestly legendary elements in the apocryphal gospels suggest that the gaps in the life of our Lord left by the scriptures were filled up rather by imagination than by an extra-scriptural tradition, and the circulation of such untrustworthy narratives must soon have made it impossible to place reliance on any story which was current but unvouched for by the canonical writers. Tradition is appealed to by the Fathers for the reception and interpretation of the Scriptures, not as source of information and saving truth flowing side by side with them.

By itself, therefore, the postulation of unrecorded beliefs does not provide a satisfactory solution of the problems connected with the development of dogma. If this is so in the case of the Assumption, where the phenomenon to be explained is merely the silence of early writing concerning a later defined dogma, it is much more so in the case of other examples of development, where early writings give testimony of the existence of beliefs contrary to, or difficult to reconcile with, the finally defined orthodoxy.[7]

7 I am indebted to Prof. G. E. M. Anscombe for criticism of this paper when presented in 1964.

II

The Nature and Existence of God

3

God and Necessity

In most times and places there have been philosophers interested in the implications of philosophical trends for religious beliefs. Contemporary England is no exception. About five years ago several groups of writers attempted to present an account of religious belief acceptable to the currently influential school of British philosophy. *New Essays in Philosophical Theology* [ed. A. G. N. Flew & A. Macintyre],[1] a collection of papers published in 1955, was followed in 1957 by two further symposia, *Faith and Logic* [ed. B. Mitchell] and *Metaphysical Beliefs* (R. W. Hepburn and others), and by Professor Ramsey's *Religious Language* and Professor Braithwaite's *An Empiricist's View of the Nature of Religious Belief*. Few readers, whether philosophers or believers, found the analyses of religious language presented in these books wholly satisfactory. I do not propose to give a summary of the views presented in these books or others which followed them. Instead, I propose to follow the fortunes of a single argument concerning natural theology which has been pursued in philosophical publications in this country during the last twenty years.

God, it is often said, is a necessary being; all else is contingent. One of Leibniz's proofs of the existence of God concludes that there exists 'a necessary Being, in whom essence involves existence, or in whom it suffices to be possible in order to be actual. Thus God

1 Throughout this article, this collection will be referred to as 'F-M'. Fuller details of the other works mentioned are given on p. 4 above.

alone (or the necessary Being) has this prerogative, that he must necessarily exist if he be possible.' Many of the philosophers whom we are considering appear to have derived their impression of natural theology either directly or indirectly from the writings of Leibniz. The attempt to understand the concept of *God* has therefore frequently taken the form of an attempt to make sense of the notion of *necessary being*. Several philosophers, finding this notion incoherent, have concluded that the concept of *God* is unintelligible.

'The only necessity that exists,' wrote Wittgenstein in the *Tractatus Logico-Philosophicus*, 'is *logical* necessity. There is no compulsion making one thing happen because another has happened' (6.37). Moreover, Wittgenstein maintained that the propositions of logic, which alone were necessary, were all tautologies; and that tautologies gave no information about the world. 'The propositions of logic are tautologies. Therefore the propositions of logic say nothing. (They are the analytic propositions)' (6.1, 6.11). Since Wittgenstein at this time accepted the thesis of *Principia Mathematica* that the whole of mathematics could be exhibited as a continuation of logic, the word 'logic' in these quotations refers also to mathematics. 'It is . . . remarkable that the infinite number of propositions of logic (mathematics) follow from half a dozen "primitive propositions". But in fact all the propositions of logic say the same thing, to wit nothing' (Ibid., 5.43).

The doctrine that the only sense of 'necessity' is 'logical necessity', and that the necessary truths of logic and mathematics were necessary only because they were tautologous, was one of the most influential theses of the *Tractatus*. The doctrine was particularly attractive to empiricists, and in particular to the logical Positivists. It enabled them to maintain, with Hume, that all our information about the world was derived from experience and contingent, without having to deny, with Mill, the *a priori* and necessary nature of mathematical truths. Tautologies say nothing about the world: logic and mathematics, if they are tautologous, are necessary only at the price of not being factual.

Thus Professor Ayer wrote in 1936 as follows:

The principles of logic and mathematics are true universally simply because we never allow them to be anything else. And the reason for this is that we cannot abandon them without contradicting ourselves, without sinning against the rules which govern the use of language, and so making our utterances self-stultifying. In other words, the truths of logic and mathematics are analytic propositions or tautologies . . . They none of them provide any information about any matter of fact. In other words they are entirely devoid of factual content. And it is for this reason that no experience can confute them. (*Language, Truth and Logic*, London, 1936, pp. 77–9)

To philosophers who think along these lines the notion of *necessary being* has naturally been a scandal. In 1942 Professor A. N. Prior published a dialogue entitled 'Can Religion be discussed?'. In this dialogue one of the characters named 'Catholic' attempts to state the difference between God and all other beings in the following manner:

What the medieval schoolmen said – and I have yet to learn that their work in this field has been improved upon – was that the Being of God is necessary, while that of all other beings is contingent. All the objects we commonly encounter can be imagined not to exist – they exist, so to speak, by chance, – but for God there is no such possibility of non-existence. He occupies the field of Being securely; his dislodgment from it is unthinkable; indeed the supposition of his dislodgment is nonsense – it cannot even be talked about; we are not really speaking of God when we say such things. God *is* his own Being. Similarly, all other beings are *what* they are 'by chance'; at least their 'properties' are contingent; one could imagine them being otherwise; all other good things, for example, even some supremely vast and good being whose vastness and goodness tempt us to worship him, are good 'by chance'; they might have been otherwise. But God couldn't have been other than good, and there is no chance of his losing his goodness; the supposition of his losing it is nonsense, because God *is* his own goodness, and all goodness. [F-M, p. 4]

Another character in the dialogue called 'Logician' criticizes this exposition as containing, in the sentence 'God is his own goodness' a confusion between abstract and common nouns. The same thing may be said, Logician concedes, either by abstract nouns or by common nouns, and either way does equally well. We may say either 'The people were very happy' or 'The people's happiness was great'. But we must opt for one method or the other. 'We cannot have it both ways, and use a word as an abstract noun and a common noun at once, as you try to do in your sentence "God is his own goodness" – that's just bad grammar, a combining of words which fails to make them *mean* – like "Cat no six" ' (F-M, p. 4). 'Catholic' is given no reply to this argument, and we are left to conclude that there is nothing to do except to call in 'Psychoanalyst' (a further character in the dialogue) to explain why people utter such meaningless jumbles of words.

Six years later, the concept of *necessary being* was criticized at greater length by Professor J. N. Findlay in a paper entitled 'Can God's Existence be disproved?' (*Mind*, 1948, reprinted in F-M). Analysis of the meaning of the word 'God', Findlay argued, could show that His existence was impossible. If God is to be an adequate object for religious attitudes, then He must be infinitely superior to His worshippers. He cannot therefore be a being which just happens to exist: His existence must be identified with His essence. His existence must be 'something inescapable and necessary, whether for thought or reality'. Moreover, He must possess in a more than accidental manner the excellences in which His creatures participate. Only if God is in some way indistinguishable from His own goodness is He worthy of *latria*. But an adequate object of worship, as described in these terms, is inconceivable.

The Divine Existence is either senseless or impossible. The modern mind feels not the faintest axiomatic force in princples which trace contingent things back to some necessarily existent source, nor does it find it hard to conceive that things should display various excellent qualities without deriving them from a source which manifests them supremely. Those who believe in necessary truths which aren't merely tautological, think that such truths merely connect the *possible* instances of various characteristics with each other; they don't expect such truths to tell us whether there *will* be instances of any characteristics. This is the outcome of the whole medieval and Kantian criticism of the Ontological Proof. And, on a yet more modern view of the matter, necessity in propositions merely reflects our use of words, the arbitrary conventions of our language. On such a view the Divine Existence could only be a necessary matter if we had made up our minds to speak theistically *whatever the empirical circumstances might turn out to be* . . . The religious frame of mind seems, in fact, to be in a quandary; it seems invincibly determined both to eat its cake and have it. It desires the Divine Existence both to have that inescapable character which can, on modern views, only be found where truth reflects an arbitrary convention, and also the character of 'making a real difference' which is only possible where truth doesn't have this merely linguistic basis. If God is to satisfy religious claims and needs, He must be a being in every way inescapable, One whose existence and whose possession of certain excellencies we cannot possibly conceive away. And modern views make it self-evidently absurd (if they don't make it ungrammatical) to speak of such a Being and attribute existence to Him. [F-M, p. 55]

In January 1949 two articles appeared in *Mind* in answer to Findlay. Professor G. E. Hughes, in the first of these, suggested that phrases like 'necessary being' and 'contingent being' were unfortunate, and thought it better to conform to modern usage by reserving the terms 'necessary' and 'contingent' to describe propositions. Restated in accordance with this restriction, Findlay's contention would be that it was self-evidently absurd to hold that 'God exists' is a necessary proposition. Findlay's proof of this conclusion was, Hughes suggested, a conflation of two arguments, neither of them convincing.

First, Findlay had argued that modern philosophical research had established that all existential propositions are necessarily contingent, and that all necessary propositions are necessarily non-existential, since they merely reflect the conventions of language. Hughes replied that the conventionalist theory was a theory merely about the propositions of logic and mathematics, and the theory that all existential propositions are contingent applied only to empirical propositions. But no theist suggested that 'God exists' was either an empirical proposition or a proposition of logic or mathematics. Even if we accept the conventionalist theory, therefore, we are not committed to saying that 'God exists' cannot be a necessary proposition. Findlay, Hughes suggested, was begging the central question, namely, whether there can be any necessary non-tautological propositions.

Secondly, Findlay appeared to argue that if God exists, then His existence must be inescapable for thought; but God's existence is not inescapable for thought, since some modern philosophers find it possible to conceive that there is no God; therefore God does not exist. Hughes retorted that this argument rested on a confusion between a proposition's being necessary and its being *seen* or *known* to be necessary. No theist had ever maintained that God's existence was inescapable in the sense that anyone who ever thought about the proposition 'God exists' found himself forced to accept it. If a proposition is necessary, then anyone who thinks clearly and who clearly understands the subject matter involved will find himself forced to accept it; and if 'God exists' is a necessary proposition, then it is in this sense inescapable. But it still does not follow that 'God exists' is self-evident even to human reason at its best: for it might be the case that the subject matter here in question was one which no human being could understand clearly enough. In fact, theists have been divided on this point. Anselm held that the proposition was self-evident to human reason at its best; Aquinas held that it was not, but was inescapable only in the sense that it was entailed by other propositions which we have sound evidence for believing to be true. Professor Findlay's 'Ontological Disproof', Hughes concluded, failed of its object. [F-M, pp. 56–64]

A more plausible argument on the same lines, Hughes suggested, would run thus. If 'God' is defined as 'necessary being', then 'God exists' becomes a tautology, since it predicates of God something already contained in the definition of God. But no tautology can be existential. Therefore 'God exists' cannot assert that God exists. Which is absurd.

This argument does not involve the contentious premise that only tautologies are necessary. None the less, Hughes maintained, it is invalid. It is true, that if 'blue', for example, were part of the definition of '*x*', then '*x* is blue' would be a tautology; but 'exists' is not a predicate like 'blue', and so the matter is different here. Professor Ryle, among others, has pointed out that if, in 'God exists', 'exists' is not a predicate, save in grammar, then, for the same reasons, in the same statement 'God' cannot be, save in grammar, the subject of predication. Hence, in Ryle's words, ' "God exists" must mean what is meant by "something and one thing only is omniscient, omnipotent, and infinitely good" (or whatever else are the characters summed up on the compound character of being a god and the only god)' (in Flew, *Logic and Language*, Oxford, 1951, pp. 15–16). So analysed, Hughes observed, the statement 'God exists' is not a tautology. The theist must maintain that, despite this, it is a necessary proposition. Findlay's argument had in no way shown this position to be untenable. Hughes concluded:

> The most that 'modern' views about such propositions can tell us about the contention that 'God exists' is a necessary proposition is that if it is we cannot here be using the term 'necessary' in quite the same sense as that in which we say that logico-mathematical propositions are necessary, and that we cannot be using the term 'exists' in quite the same way as when we say that tables and chairs exist. But these are statements with which the theist need have no quarrel. [F-M, p. 67]

Another theist critic of Findlay, Mr A. C. A. Rainer, was prepared, unlike Hughes, to deny that 'God exists' was a necessary proposition. He wrote as follows:

> The necessity of God's existence is not the same as the necessity of a logical implication. It means, for those who believe in it, God's complete actuality, indestructibility, *aseitas*

or independence of limiting conditions. It is a property ascribed to God, not a property of our assertion about God . . . For us, both the assertion of God's necessary existence and the assertion of his necessary possession of the properties of a Perfect Being are contingent. [F-M, p. 69][2]

To say that God cannot exist necessarily because we cannot necessarily assert his existence, Rainer concluded, was to commit the converse fallacy of Anselm's ontological argument.

Findlay's reply to his critics in *Mind* (1949) was surprisingly irenic. His argument, he said, was not so modern after all: it was merely a development of Kant's criticism of the Ontological Argument.

> Kant said that it couldn't be necessary that there should ever *be* anything of any description whatsoever, and that *if* we included 'existence' in the definition of something – Kant of course didn't think we *should* so include it, as existence 'wasn't a predicate' – we could only say, *hypothetically*, that *if* something of a certain sort existed, then it *would* exist necessarily, but not, categorically, that it actually existed. And he also said that if one were willing to deny the existence of God one couldn't be compelled to assert any property of him, no matter how intimately such a property formed part of his 'nature'. Now, Kant, of course, didn't make existence (or necessary existence) part of God's nature, but I have argued that one *ought* to do so, if God is to be the adequate object of our religious attitudes. So that for all those who are willing to accept *my* account of an adequate religious object, and also Kant's doctrine of the hypothetical character of necessary predications, it must follow inevitably that there cannot be an adequate object for our religious attitudes [F-M, pp. 72–3].

He considered, however, that there was perhaps little difference between the position of a theist who thought that God existed in a

---

2 I. M. Crombie agreed with Rainer that 'God exists' is a contingent proposition (F-M, pp. 113–4).

sense of the word different from the ordinary sense, and his own attitude of unquestioning reverence to an imaginary ideal. 'When theists say,' he concluded, 'that their God exists in some sense quite different from created objects, there seems but a hairsbreadth between them and such atheists as place their ideal, with Plato and Plotinus, ἐπέκεινα τῆς οὐσίας' [F-M, p. 74].

In 1955 views similar to Findlay's were expressed in a public lecture at the University of Adelaide by Professor J. J. C. Smart. Smart in this lecture presented and criticized various arguments for God's existence. He presented the cosmological argument as follows:

> Everything in the world around is *contingent*. That is, with regard to any particular thing, it is quite conceivable that it might not have existed. For example, if you were asked why you existed, you could say that it was because of your parents, and if asked why they existed you could go still further back, but however far you go back you have not, so it is argued, made the fact of your existence really intelligible. For however far back you go in such a series you only get back to something which itself might not have existed. For a really satisfying explanation of why anything contingent (such as you or me or this table) exists you must eventually begin with something which is not itself contingent, that is, with something of which we cannot say that it might not have existed, that is we must begin with a necessary being. [F-M, pp. 35–6]

'Necessary being' in this context, according to Smart, means the same as 'Logically necessary being'. A logically necessary being is a being whose non-existence is inconceivable in the sort of way that a triangle's having four sides is inconceivable. But the concept of such a being is a self-contradictory concept. For since 'necessary' is a predicate of propositions and not of things, 'God is a necessary being' must mean the same as 'The proposition "God exists" is logically necessary'. But necessary propositions – such as '3 + 2 = 5', 'a thing cannot be red and green all over', 'either it is raining or it is not raining' – are guaranteed solely by the rules for the use of the symbols they contain. It follows that no existential proposition can be logically necessary.

The truth of a logically necessary proposition depends only on our symbolism, or to put the same thing in another way, on the relationship of concepts . . . [But] an existential proposition does not say that one concept is involved in another, but that a concept applies to something. An existential proposition must be very different from any logically necessary one, such as a mathematical one, for example, for the conventions of our symbolism clearly leave it open for us either to affirm or deny an existential proposition; it is not our symbolism but reality which decides whether or not we must affirm it or deny it. The claim that the existence of God should be *logically* necessary is thus a self-contradictory one. [F-M, pp. 38–9]

The necessity of God, therefore, is not a logical necessity. Instead, Smart prefers to say that God's existence is a 'religious necessity' by which he means that 'it would clearly upset the structure of our religious attitudes in the most violent way if we denied it or even entertained the possibility of its falsehood' [F-M, p. 40].

The essays of Findlay and Smart were republished in 1955 in the symposium *New Essays in Philosophical Theology* [F-M]. In a review of this book Professor Raphael Demos used against the critics of necessary being an argument of a pattern familiar in anti-positivist polemic. What was the status, he asked, of the proposition 'Only analytic propositions are necessary'? If it is analytic, then it merely records Smart and Findlay's determination to use certain terms in a particular way. If it is meant to be an inductive generalization, then the statement 'God exists' which is claimed as an exception, must be examined on its own merits and not rejected *a priori*. There is no third alternative for Findlay and Smart, since they are committed to excluding the possibility of necessary synthetic propositions.[3]

Demos commented that it was ironical that Findlay and Smart should attack the notion of necessary being in the name of contemporary philosophy: for the distinction between analytic and synthetic propositions, on which their attack was based, had

3 'The meaningfulness of religious language' *Philosophy & Phenomenological Research* (1957), pp. 96–106.

recently been called in question by influential philosophers of the school to which they appealed.[4]

The basis of the criticism of the notion of necessary being was indeed increasingly called in question. Prior, with whose criticisms this discussion began, published in 1953 a paper with the title 'Is necessary existence possible?' in which he attacked the thesis that the only necessity is logical necessity. (*Philosophy and Phenomenological Research* (1955), pp. 45–47).

The line of argument to prove that 'necessary being' is a senseless phrase, Prior observed, starts from the position that existence is not a predicate. What is not rightly thought of as attaching to a subject at all is not rightly thought of as attaching to a subject necessarily. But the belief that existence is not a predicate, Prior now wished to contend, is perfectly compatible with the belief that 'necessary existence' makes sense.

Prior accepted the customary analysis of existential propositions which derived from Moore. According to this analysis, 'Lions exist' asserts that the concept of *lionhood* is exemplified, and 'unicorns do not exist' that the concept of *unicornhood* is not exemplified. Now one can distinguish between the necessary and contingent non-exemplification of concepts: it is contingent that *unicornhood* is not exemplified, it is necessary that *non-cubical cubicity* is unexemplified.

Why should there not be a similar distinction, Prior asked, between *exemplified* concepts? Since there are properties of concepts which preclude their exemplification, why should there not also be properties of concepts which necessitate their exemplification? Prior admitted that he did not know of any such necessarily exemplified concept: he rejected the suggestion that self-complementariness (the property of *being x or not being x*) might be such a concept. Someone might propose the property of *exemplification* for the role. To this proposal Prior replied as follows:

> We must reply that that is not the sort of necessitation intended; and to indicate what *is* intended, we may simply say that we are using 'necessitates' in such a sense that to say that '*B* is necessitated by *A*' is in some way to account for *B*.

4 See, for example, Quine, *From a Logical Point of View* (Cambridge, 1953).

Logical necessitation will not do here – you do not account for
X's being Y by saying that X's being Y necessitates X's being
Y, though this in a sense is true. And logical necessity, I
should further contend, is itself to be defined in terms of this
other sort. To say that A is a logically necessary proposition is
to say that A's truth is (pre-logically) necessitated by its
logical form.

The recognition of another sort of necessity alongside, and prior
to logical necessity, marks a departure from the *Tractatus* doctrine
that the only necessity is logical necessity. Recently, Professor
Kneale has pointed out that the *Tractatus* itself contains elements
which contradict this doctrine. In one place Wittgenstein explained
negation in the following manner: 'The negating statement
determines a logical place *other* than that determined by the
negated statement. The negating statement determines a logical
place with the help of the logical place of the negated statement, by
describing it as lying outside this latter' (4.0641). This implies,
Kneale observes, that the possibility of using a negative particle
significantly depends on the objective incompatibility of various
thinkable states of affairs. For the otherness here spoken of is
presupposed by the construction of negative statements and must
therefore be a relation independent of our use of a negative sign. In
fact, inconsistency of general terms presupposes incompatibility of
characters; and from this it follows that necessity cannot be merely
a product of linguistic rules and customs. (W. & M. Kneale, *The
Development of Logic* Oxford, 1963 pp. 633–9)
   Ayer himself, in the introduction to the second edition of
Language, Truth and Logic, had recanted his former account of *a priori*
truth.

I now think that it is a mistake to say that they [*a priori*
propositions] are themselves linguistic rules. For apart from
the fact that they can properly be said to be true, which
linguistic rules cannot, they are distinguished also by being
necessary, whereas linguistic rules are arbitrary. At the same
time, if they are necessary it is only because the relevant
linguistic rules are presupposed . . . In Russell's and White-

head's system of logic, it is a contingent, empirical fact that the sign '⊃' should have been given the meaning that it has, and the rules which govern the use of this sign are conventions, which themselves are neither true nor false; but given these rules the *a priori* proposition '$p.\supset.q\supset p$' is necessarily true. Being *a priori*, this proposition gives no information in the ordinary sense in which an empirical proposition may be said to give information, nor does it itself prescribe how the logical constant '⊃' is to be used. (p. 17)

The necessity of logical truths is thus put forward as being the consequence of, and not identical with, the adoption of a set of rules. But this consequence is itself necessary: it is not a contingent fact that, given the relevant rules, '$q.\supset.p\supset q$' is necessarily true. And this consequence is itself necessary only in virtue of what Prior called 'pre-logical necessity'. It is, as Ayer says, an empirical fact that the symbol '⊃' has been given the meaning that it has; and the rules for its use are based on a convention. But it is not because of any further convention that, given '⊃' has the use it has, '$q.\supset.p\supset q$' is true; nor is it an empirical fact that the convention for the use of '⊃' is one which it is possible to make.

The doctrine that necessary propositions are merely uninformative byproducts of our linguistic conventions thus proves impossible to uphold. Kneale has suggested that the popularity of the doctrine is due to its being a distorted version of an important truth about *a priori* knowledge:

Anything we come to know *a priori* is a second-order truth about the relations of propositions or a truism derivative from such a truth, and in either case it is learnt by reflection on the meaning of words or other symbols. An animal such as a dog may perhaps be said to know a contingent fact such as that there are two sheep in a field, but it seems absurd to say that a dog can know even a very simple truth of arithmetic such as the proposition that $2 + 2 = 4$; and the reason can scarcely be that all non-human animals lack the special kind of intuition which according to Kant enables us to learn arithmetical truths. Many misleading accounts of *a priori* knowledge have been inspired by Plato's notion of contemplation (θεωρία) as a kind of intellectual gazing in which the soul may read off facts about super-sensible objects; and if we are to free ourselves from the influence of these it is no doubt important that we should realize the connection of *a priori* knowledge with the use of symbols. (p. 636)

It is possible to agree with Kneale that all *a priori* truths are learnt by what Mill called 'the artful manipulation of language', without following him in his belief that all *a priori* truths are truths *about* the symbols of a language. In arithmetic, for example, it seems *prima facie* that by manipulating numerals and other symbols we come to know truths about numbers which are not themselves symbols. And Kneale himself elsewhere writes as if this were the case.[5]

So far, in this paper, I have not made any division between necessary propositions of different kinds. I have written as if the terms 'analytic', '*a priori*', 'necessary' and 'tautological' were, if not synonymous, at least coextensive in application. In this I have followed some of the authors whose discussion of *necessary being* it has been my purpose to record. It is time now to draw some necessary distinctions.

The term 'analytic' was given currency by Kant. The judgement that *A* is *B* is analytic, according to Kant, if the predicate *B* belongs to the subject *A* as something which is contained in the concept *A*; otherwise it is synthetic. Kant's dichotomy as it stands applies to judgments, and not to propositions, and among judgements applies only to those of subject-predicate form. If we wish to give it application to propositions of various forms, we do better to take a different definition of 'analytic' – one which is nowhere put forward by Kant, but which is implicit in the use which he makes of the term. We may say that a true proposition is analytic if, and only if, its negation is self-contradictory.

Some analytic propositions are tautologies in the strict sense in which Wittgenstein introduced this term into logic. In this sense, a tautology is a compound proposition which is true no matter what

5 See the passage referred to on page 51 below: W. & M. Kneale, *The Development of Logic*, p. 707.

may be the truth-values of the propositions which enter into its composition. All tautologies are analytically true by the definition given. But not all propositions which are analytically true are tautologies. 'Either some Greeks are philosophers or none are', 'All actresses are female', 'Three o'clock comes one hour after two o'clock' are all analytically true propositions. But none of them is a tautology.

The notion of *tautology* and the distinction between analytic and synthetic truths is a distinction belonging to the field of logic. The distinction between *a priori* truths and *a posteriori* truths, on the other hand, is drawn from theory of knowledge or epistemology. *A priori* truths are truths which are known on logical grounds alone; *a posteriori* truths are truths which are known only by experience. It is being increasingly recognized that not all *a priori* truths are analytic. Kneale lists several examples of such truths which are not analytic.[6]

> An example which has often been discussed is the proposition that nothing can be both red and green all over at the same time. Another is the proposition that the relation of temporal precedence is transitive but irreflexive. Furthermore, if we can ever be sure that certain perceptible characters and relations provide a model satisfying the postulates of an abstract geometry, this too must be a piece of knowledge *a priori* but not analytic. (p. 637)

No analytic proposition is existential. A denial of existence can never be self-contradictory. But since the class of logically true propositions is wider than that of analytic propositions, it does not follow that no existential proposition can be established *a priori*. The thesis that there are no logically true existential propositions has, indeed, long been popular. As Kneale has observed, it can be quite easily refuted by the production of counter-examples from mathematics. It is not a fact of experience that there is a prime

6 Kneale's definition of 'analytic' is broader than the one I have given; but any proposition which is not analytic in Kneale's sense is *a fortiori* not analytic in my sense.

number greater than a million. Someone might object, as Kneale himself, in another mood, appears to do, that such a truth is really a second-order truth about the relations between propositions, and does not deal with 'real existence' as empirical existential propositions do. If so, then the objector must give some account of the difference between real and non-real existence. The presence or absence of an existential quantifier can no longer be regarded as the criterion of whether a proposition is really existential.

The distinctions which I have just drawn were sometimes denied, and sometimes ignored, by the authors whom we have been considering. Only when they have been drawn can one fruitfully consider the meaning of the terms 'necessary' and 'contingent' as applied to propositions. We must first ask whether the dichotomy between necessary and contingent corresponds to the dichotomy between analytic and synthetic, or to the dichotomy between *a priori* and *a posteriori*, or to neither of those dichotomies. In this field, the ground was usefully cleared in 1958 by Mr Richard Robinson in an essay entitled 'Necessary Propositions'. (*Mind*, LXVII (1958), pp. 289–384).

Robinson distinguished four senses in which propositions have been called 'necessary'. by 'a necessary proposition' one may mean:

1   A proposition which one cannot not believe.
2   An apodeictic modal proposition.
3   An analytic proposition.
4   An unrestrictedly general universal proposition.

Each of these senses is independent of each of the others: a proposition may be necessary in one of these sense without being necessary in any of the other senses.

Used in any of these senses, Robinson suggests, the word 'necessary' has a perfectly clear meaning. Leibniz, for instance, used it in the third sense. He wrote: 'A truth is necessary when the opposite implies contradiction, and when it is not necessary it is called contingent.' A necessary truth, he seems to mean, is a truth whose contradictory is self-contradictory. This is the definition which, we have seen, best fits Kant's use of the word 'analytic' when the concept of *necessary proposition* has become thoroughly muddled. Robinson illustrates the confusion from Kant's writings, and concludes: 'Kant thought he had found a necessary proposition whenever he felt compelled to believe (sense 1) a proposition which either asserted that something *must* be so (sense 2) or had a self-contradictory (sense 3), or asserted something with unrestricted universality (sense 4).'

One confusion which is still prevalent concerns the relationship between necessity and truth. Is a necessary proposition by definition a true one? If we take 'necessary' in the first, second or fourth sense, we must admit that some necessary propositions are false. Some of the propositions which some people cannot help believing are false; some propositions which say that something *must* be so are false; some propositions which say that something universally *is* so are false. But if we say that an analytic proposition is one whose contradictory is self-contradictory, then all propositions which are necessary in the third of the senses listed above are true.

To avoid confusion, Robinson suggests that we define analytic propositions as those of which either the assertion or the denial is self-contradictory. Thus, the pairs of terms 'analytic/synthetic' and 'necessary/contingent' in all their senses, will divide *all* propositions, and not only *true* propositions.

It is only in its third sense that Robinson takes 'necessary' seriously as a useful term in philosophy. He introduces his other three senses only for purposes of illustrating and pruning the confusions which he detects in Kant. Accordingly, he is left with two pairs of terms, 'analytic/synthetic' and 'necessary/contingent' to refer to a single distinction. He ends with a plea, on aesthetic grounds, that the distinction be marked by the terms 'necessary' and 'contingent' rather than their alternatives.

I shall follow Robinson in dismissing, for our present purposes, the first, second, and fourth of the listed senses of 'necessary'. I shall not, however, follow his proposal that we should use 'necessary' only as an elegant synonym for 'analytic'. For the rest of this essay I shall continue to use 'analytic' in the sense defined, since I believe that there are senses of 'necessary' other than those listed by Robinson which are of philosophical importance.

In the first place, most people would agree that all logical truths are necessary truths, and that whatever is *a priori* false is necessarily false. But if, as we have seen reason to believe, there are *a priori* propositions which are not analytic, then there are some necessary propositions which are not analytic.

If this were all, however, the distinction between necessary and contingent propositions would still be superfluous. 'Necessary', though no longer a synonym for 'analytic', would become simply an elegant variant of '*a priori*'. But given the current view of the nature of propositions, I think we can go no farther. Kneale suggests that there may be necessary truths which are not truths which can be known *a priori*; not because they can be known *a posteriori* but because they cannot be known at all. He writes: 'It does not seem absurd to suggest that there may be necessary truths about unperceived qualities or relations which no one can ever know because (as Locke might say) no one has the requisite ideas' (*The Development of Logic*, p. 637). In this context he defines necessary truths as 'truths without alternatives'. It is difficult to make sense of this unless 'necessary truth' means the same as 'necessarily true proposition'. But if it does, then it is hard to see how what is here said can be reconciled with Kneale's view that the word 'proposition' refers to the common feature of actual or possibile utterances that resemble each other completely as vehicles of communication (p. 593). A possible utterance is an utterance which somebody can make. Nobody can make an utterance if he has not the ideas requisite for its making. If there are ideas which nobody *can* have, then no utterances are possible which presuppose such ideas: there are, therefore, no corresponding propositions. If, on the other hand, the ideas which Kneale postulates are ideas which *can* be acquired, but which nobody in fact possesses, then the truth of the propositions in question *can* be known also, provided only that the ideas have first been acquired. On the view of propositions which Kneale accepts, therefore, no difference has been made out between *a priori* propositions and necessary propositions.

If, however, we reject the current doctrine that no proposition can change its truth-value, then it becomes possible to use the words 'necessary' and 'contingent' to mark a distinction which is not marked by any other pair of terms. For we may say that a contingent proposition is a proposition which *can* change its truth-value, and a necessary proposition is one which *cannot* change its truth-value. On this view, all analytic and *a priori* propositions are necessary, for analytic truths and logical truths are always true, while self-contradictory statements and *a priori* falsehoods are always false. But the converse does not hold: not all propositions which are necessary in this sense are either analytic or *a priori*.

On the current theory of the nature of the proposition, no proposition can be at one time true and at another false. A sentence such as 'Theaetetus is sitting', which is true when Theaetetus is sitting, and false at other times, would now commonly be said to express a different proposition at different times, so that at one time it expresses a true proposition, and at another time a false one. And a sentence asseting that 'Theaetetus is sitting' *was true* at time *t* is now commonly treated as asserting that the proposition which ascribes *sitting at time t* to Theaetetus is true timelessly. No proposition is significantly tensed, but any proposition expressed by a tensed sentence contains a reference to time and is itself timelessly true or false.

There is another way of looking at a proposition, which was classically expressed in Aristotle's *De Interpretatione*. On this account, a sentence such as 'Theaetetus is sitting' *is* a proposition, in the sense in which a particular piece of shaped metal is a shilling. This proposition is significantly tensed, and is at some times true and at others false. It becomes true whenever Theaetetus sits down, and becomes false whenever Theaetetus ceases to sit.

Arguments have been put forward recently to show that this second account of the nature of the proposition is to be preferred to the one now common.[7] I shall not now discuss whether these arguments are convincing. What here concerns us is that the *De Interpretatione* view was the one accepted by those Aristotelian philosophers who traditionally described God as a necessary being. It is impossible to make sense of this notion without taking seriously the possibility of propositions changing their truth value.

If we accept the view that mathematics does not concern itself with real existence, then we must admit that the modern criticisms

7 Notably by Prior in *Time and Modality* (Oxford, 1957).

we have been considering establish that it is absurd to say that 'God exists' is an analytic or *a priori* proposition. The Leibnizian notion of *necessary being* must therefore be abandoned. It remains to be seen whether 'God exists' can be said to be necessary in the Aristotelian sense, and whether the Aristotelian notion of *necessary being* may be preserved.[8]

God is, by definition, eternal: those who believe in God believe that He is and always was and always will be. A being, however magnificent, which came into existence or which passed away would not be God. It follows that 'God exists' is a necessary proposition by our new definition of 'necessary'. For if 'God exists' is true, then it always has been true and always will be true. And if 'God exists' is false, then it always has been false and always will be false. The proposition 'God exists', whether true or false, cannot change its truth-value. By our definition, therefore, it is a necessary proposition. Furthermore, since God possesses His attributes unchangingly, 'God is good', 'God knows whatever is to be known' and 'God the Father loves God the Son' are all necessary propositions. But not only propositions about God are necessary by our criterion. Apart from *a priori* propositions, any propositions, true or false, ascribing everlasting existence are necessary. When Aristotelians stated that the heavenly bodies were eternal, and when Lucretius claimed everlasting existence for his atoms, they asserted propositions which, by our criterion were necessary.

It was pointed out by Rainer that when scholastics said that God was a necessary being they meant that He was eternal and imperishable. It is because God is necessary in this sense, that the proposition 'God exists' is necessary in the sense we have defined. The necessity *de dicto*, the medievals would have said, follows from the necessity *de re*: the property of the proposition about God derives from the property of the concept of *being God*. With

8 In calling this notion 'Aristotelian' I mean no more than that it is a notion implicit in discussions of necessity by Aristotelian philosophers. For a fuller and documented account of the topics treated in this last part, see my article 'Necessary Being' (p. 60). Aristotle's own doctrine of necessity is complicated by the fact that, believing that what can happen sometimes does happen, he was committed to the belief that what is always true is necessarily true.

Leibnizian necessary being, the converse was the case: a supposititious property was ascribed to God on the basis of an alleged property (e.g. self-evidence) of the proposition 'God exists'.

Again, when it is said that God possesses His attributes necessarily, no more need be meant than that God is wholly unchangeable. How then are we to take those expressions – such as 'God is His wisdom' – which Prior found so puzzling in the essay with which we began?

The most satisfactory modern treatment of them is that given by Mr Geach in his account of Aquinas' theory of *form*.[9] Geach insists that when Aquinas speaks of 'form' he is not referring to any entity such as 'that of which "wisdom" is a proper name'; for Aquinas was no Platonist, and without Platonism one cannot admit that 'wisdom' is a proper name at all. Nor, strictly speaking, would 'the wisdom of Socrates' stand for a form: for Aquinas says that forms are as such multipliable. 'The wisdom of Socrates' does not mean: wisdom, which Socrates possesses. 'Of' does not denote a special relation of possessing. Geach suggests that the phrase should be divided into two members thus: 'The wisdom of . . .' and 'Socrates.' It is a phrase such as 'The wisdom of . . .' which best expresses what Aquinas had in mind when he talked of forms: this is what he meant when he said that a form was *entis* and not *ens* – it must be followed by a genitive. (*Summa Theologiae*, Ia, 45, 4)

Geach here draws an analogy from mathematics. 'The square root of 4' does not refer to an entity called 'the square root' which stands in the relation *belonging to* to the number 4. Logically, the phrase must be divided 'The square root of/4': the first part of the phrase, which is to be followed by some number-expression or other, is the sign of a *function*; and the numeral '4' completes this function-sign with the sign of an *argument*. 'The wisdom of Socrates' is not a form *simpliciter*, but a form *of Socrates*, just as 2 is not the square-root function, but is that function *of 4*.

Applying this to the doctrine of God's 'simplicity', Geach writes:

When Aquinas says things like *Deus est ipsa sapientia* he is not meaning that God is that of which the name 'wisdom' is a

9 'Form and existence', *Proceedings of the Aristotelian Society*, 55 (1955), pp. 251–72.

proper name, for the Platonists are wrong in thinking that there is such an object, and Aquinas says they are wrong. But we can take it to mean that 'God' and 'the wisdom of God' are two names of the same thing . . . for we can significantly say that 'God' and 'the wisdom of God' and 'the power of God' are three names with the same reference; but 'the wisdom of . . .' and 'the power of . . .' have not the same reference, any more than the predicates 'wise' and 'powerful' have.

Here again, the mathematical analogy is helpful. 'The square of . . .' and 'the double of . . .' signify two quite different functions, but for the argument 2 these two functions both take the number 4 as their value. Similarly 'the wisdom of . . .' and 'the power of . . .' signify different forms, but the individualizations of these forms in God's case are not distinct from one another; nor is either distinct from God, just as the number 1 is in no way distinct from its own square.

It does not seem to have been shown, therefore, that the notion of *necessary being* employed by the medieval scholastics is an incoherent one. In spite of Kant, if our argument has been correct, it is possible to accept a proof of God's existence from the things He has made without being committed to an acceptance of the manifest fallacy of the Ontological Argument.

The following argument is sometimes used against the possibility of any proof that there is a God. Such a proof must either contain only *a priori* premises, or must contain in addition to *a priori* premises some *a posteriori* ones. If the former, it can prove nothing about real existence. If the latter, then the existence of God will be at best a revisable empirical hypothesis.

In fact, the traditional causal demonstrations of the existence of God claimed to start from indubitable premises (e.g. 'some things change') and proceed according to the normal rules of logic to the conclusion that there is a God. Such a proof, if valid, would lead to an indubitable conclusion: 'there is a God', if proved by such means, would be no more a revisable hypothesis than 'some things change' is. On the other hand, 'some things change' is not *a priori true*; so there is no difficulty in principle about this premise leading to a conclusion concerning real existence.

The Five Ways of St Thomas Aquinas were supposed to be proofs of just this sort. Whether any of them is valid, I do not know. No serious work on them has been done by philosophers of the school we are considering. Philosophers have frequently been led to believe that work on them would be a waste of time by the erroneous opinion that the type of being whose existence they professed to establish was a self-contradictory *Unding*. I hope that this essay has done something to show that the impression is mistaken.[10]

10 Some prolegomena to a consideration of the Five Ways are put forward by Geach in 'Causality and creation' *Sophia*, 1 (1962), pp. 1–8.

4

Necessary Being

God, it is often said, is a necessary being; all else is contingent. One of Leibniz's proofs for the existence of God concludes that there exists 'a necessary Being, in whom essence involves existence, or in whom it suffices to be possible in order to be actual. Thus God alone (or the necessary Being) has this prerogative, that he must necessarily exist if he be possible'. If God is a necessary being in this sense, then 'there is a God' is a logically necessary proposition. Many recent writers have argued that no proposition concerning real existence can be either analytic or *a priori* true. The notion of such a necessary being, they have concluded, is self-contradictory. I do not intend in this paper to question such criticisms. Instead, I intend to explore a wider notion of propositional necessity, and to discuss a sense of 'necessary being' other than that of Leibniz.

Aquinas, like Leibniz, held that God was a necessary being (*Summa Theologiae*, Ia, 2, 3c etc.). Unlike Leibniz, he believed that God was not the only necessary being (*Summa contra Gentes*, II, 30 etc.). Like Leibniz, however, he believed that only in God did essence and existence coincide (*De Veritate*, 10, 12c). If he was consistent, therefore, Aquinas did not mean by 'a necessary being' a being in whom essence involves existence.

Aquinas defines '*necessarium*' as meaning the same as '*quod non potest non esse*' (*3 Sent.* 16, 1, 2c). Thus, a proposition is necessary if it cannot not be true (S. T. Ia, 1, 44 ,1 ad 2). A substance is necessary if it cannot not exist (S. c. G. II, 30). An event is necessary if it cannot not take place (S. c. G. I, 84). Because 'be true', 'exist' and 'take place' can all appear in Latin as '*esse*', Aquinas in discussion leaps from the necessity of propositions to the necessity of things and events in a manner which is often disconcerting (e.g. *In VIII Phys*, 3).

Let us consider first necessity in propositions. What can it mean to say that a proposition cannot not be true? If we do not allow that a proposition may change its truth-value, then there is no room for a distinction between a proposition's *being true* and *being able to be true*. Most philosophers nowadays regard a proposition as some-thing, expressed by a sentence, to which one or other of the predicates 'true' or 'false' once for all applies. On such a view, one and the same type-sentence (or indeed one and the same token-sentence, such as an inscription) may express now a true proposition, now a false proposition, at another time perhaps no proposition at all. Such a sentence may be said to become true, to be true for a certain length of time, and to cease to be true. But any proposition which it expresses is itself either perpetually true or perpetually false. No proposition, whether analytic or synthetic, whether *a priori* or *a posteriori*, can have any truth-value other than that which it now has, has always had, and always will have (e.g. W. & M. Kneale, *The Development of Logic*, pp. 49–54).

Accordingly, there is no room, on the current view of the nature of the proposition, for a distinction between necessarily true propositions and merely *de facto* true propositions, on the basis of the possibility or non-possibility of a change in their truth-value. We might think, perhaps, that we can distinguish between propositions such as analytic propositions which *have to be* true, and propositions about matters of fact which, though perpetually true, *might have been* false. But when we say that something *might have been* we mean that there was some time when there was a genuine possibility that it might be. Gaitskell might have become Prime Minister in 1961 because in 1961 'Gaitskell may become Prime Minister this year' was true. But if '*p*' is true, then, on the Kneale's view, there never was a time when '*p* may become false' was true. And this, no matter whether '*p*' is analytic or matter-of-fact.

We might well wonder why the terms 'necessary' and 'contingent' have continued to be applied to propositions since it became common practice to regard truth-values of propositions as unchangeable. Richard Robinson, in an instructive article in *Mind* (1958, pp. 289ff.) has shown that since Kant much of the use of the terms has been the product of confusion. Robinson himself suggests that the only philosophically respectable use of the word 'necessary' is as a synonym for 'analytic', where an analytic proposition is taken to be a proposition of which either the assertion or the denial is self-contradictory. If, like the Kneales, we believe in synthetic *a priori* propositions, we shall no doubt wish to call these also 'necessary propositions'. But, on either account, 'necessary' in this context is no more than an elegant variant for 'analytic' or '*a priori*'.

It is open to someone who takes the modern view of the nature of the proposition to say that 'necessary' and 'contingent' are predicates which apply to sentences, not to propositions. We can certainly draw a distinction, using the modern terminology, between a sentence such as 'cabbages are vegetables' which always expresses a true proposition, and a sentence such as 'cabbages are cheap' which sometimes expresses a true proposition and sometimes a false proposition. We can distinguish too between sentences such as 'this man is an actor' which may, in an appropriate context, express a true proposition, and sentences such as 'this man is an actress' which can never, in any circumstances, express a true proposition. There is thus room within the modern system to employ the terms 'necessary' and 'contingent' to make a distinction other than that between *a priori* and *a posteriori* propositions.

I shall not now explore this possibility: I shall take the alternative course of admitting the possibility of change in the truth-value of a proposition. This was the course which was taken in the middle ages. By '*propositio*', medieval logicians did not mean something which was expressed by a propositional sign. Rather, they meant the propositional sign itself, considered not as a set of sounds or marks, but as the utterance of an intelligent being. On this account, a sentence *is* a proposition, in somewhat the sense in which a particular piece of shaped metal *is* a shilling.

On the modern view, no proposition is tensed. On the medieval view, a proposition such 'Theaetetus is sitting' is significantly tensed, and is at some times true and at others false. It becomes true whenever Theaetetus sits down, and becomes false whenever Theaetetus ceases to sit. In looking at the matter thus, the medievals were following Aristotle (*Categories*, 5, 4a, 23–6).

Aquinas, like other medieval logicians, accepted the possibility of change in the truth-value of a proposition (S. T. Ia, 19, 5 ad 3). If we follow him in this, then it seems that we can draw a distinction between those true propositions which can cease to be true, and those which cannot cease to be true. Theaetetus is sitting, but there is nothing to prevent him standing up; 'Theaetetus is sitting' is true, but at any moment it may become false. On the other hand, '2 + 2 = 4' is true, has always been true, always will be true, and can never cease to be true. We might mark this distinction by the pair of terms 'contingent' and 'necessary'. In doing so, we would be applying to the particular case of propositional truth the definition of 'necessary' as 'what cannot not be'. A proposition is necessarily true if it cannot not be true; is necessarily false if it cannot not be false; and is necessary if it is either necessarily true or necessarily false.

It is obvious enough that all analytic propositions and all *a priori* propositions will be necessary propositions on this definition. 'It is raining and it is not raining' and 'Theaetetus is red and green all over' cannot become true; 'There is a prime number greater than a million' and 'All elephants are animals' cannot become false. But not all propositions which are necessary by our new criterion are either analytic or *a priori*. Any proposition ascribing perpetual existence, or purporting to describe an unchangeable state of affairs, will now count as necessary. When Lucretius claimed everlasting existence for his atoms, he was stating a proposition which was in this sense necessary.

The sense of 'necessity' introduced is obviously much wider than that of 'logical necessity'. Polythene, I am told, is indestructible. If this is literally so, then 'polythene exists' is a necessary truth; but it is not a logically necessary truth. It is impossible to decide from considerations of logic alone whether 'polythene exists' is true, or whether it is necessary. On the other hand, there are proposition whose truth can be settled only by inquiry into the facts, but whose necessity can be known on logical grounds alone. 'The sun will always exist' is a case in point: if it is true, it can never cease to be true; if it is false, it can never cease to be false.

Among propositions which are in this way logically necessary but not logically true are many propositions about God. God is, by definition, eternal: those who believe in God believe that He is and always was and always will be. A being, however magnificent, who came into existence or who passed away, would not be God. It follows that 'God exists' is a necessary proposition: for if it is true, then it cannot ever become false; and if it is false, it cannot ever become true. One can believe that 'God exists' is necessary in this sense without believing that it is analytic, or logically true, or true at all. So too with 'God is wise' and 'God knows all that is to be known'.

On this view of necessity, the necessity of the proposition 'God exists' depends on a property of God, namely, his eternity. This is in contrast to the Leibnizian view, on which necessity is a property ascribed to God on the basis of an alleged property (*viz.* self-evidence) of the proposition 'God exists'.

The definition of 'necessary proposition' here discussed was suggested by Aquinas' definition of '*necessarium*' as '*quod non potest non esse*'. Aquinas' use of 'necesary' with propositions corresponds on the whole to the use which we have introduced. He distinguishes between absolute and conditional necessity; but even the class of absolutely necessary propositions includes many propositions which are obviously not logically necessary, such as *esse alternationem noctis et diei*. He expressly distinguishes such causal necessities from a proposition such as *triangulum habere tres angulos aequales duobus rectis* which, he believed, was necessarily true because it could be derived from the definition of a triangle (*In II Phys* 15).

Like Aristotle, Aquinas believed that all past-tensed propositions about matters of fact were necessary (S. T. Ia 14, 13 ad 2). In this he seems to have been mistaken, if he was using 'necessary' in the sense which we have suggested; but the mistake is a very natural one. There are many past-tensed propositions which on the definition given are necessary. 'Nero fiddled while Rome burnt', if it is true, will always be true; if it is false, it is too late now for it to come true. So 'Nero fiddled while Rome burnt' cannot change its truth-value and is a necessary proposition in this sense. But it is not true of all past-tensed propositions that they cannot change their truth-value. An affirmative past-tensed proposition which contains no reference to a definite time, if true, must remain true; but if false, it may become true. The corresponding negative past-tensed proposition, on the other hand, if true, may become false; but if false, it must remain false. For what has happened cannot not have happened; but what has not yet happened may yet happen. As I write this, 'Kenny has published an article in *Sophia*' is false; by the time you read it it will have become true. On the other hand 'Kenny has not published an article in *Sophia*' is, as I write, true; when you read it it will be false. Neither of these past-tensed propositions, then, is necessary at the time of writing; but by the time you read them each of them will have become necessary. For a past-tensed proposition of this kind, having once changed its truth-value, can do so no more.

It is by now obvious that the distinction which we have drawn is a pretty freakish one. There seems something very wrong with a definition of 'necessary' which makes at one and the same time 'Nero fiddled while Rome burnt' necessary and 'Kenny has published an article in *Sophia*' contingent; and which makes one and the same proposition change from one side to the other of the dichotomy in the course of its history. By implication, there is something wrong also with Aquinas' use of *necessarium* as applied to propositions. Before seeing if anything can be done to remedy this, I will turn to what Aquinas says about the necessity of substances.

In his Third Way to prove the existence of God (S. T. Ia, 2, 3c; S. c. G. I, 15) Aquinas divides beings into two classes, *possibilia* and *necessaria*. *Possibilia* are beings '*quae sunt possibilia esse et non esse*': namely '*generabilia et corruptibilia*', beings which *come from* other things and *turn into* other things, as an animal comes from its parents and turns into dust. *Necessaria*, by contrast, are beings which do not come from anything and which cannot turn into anything. Aquinas offers a (fallacious) proof that not everything is *possibile*: he concludes that there must be at least one necessary being. But he does not go on to say 'and this all men call "God" '; instead, he draws a further distinction between *necessaria quae habent causam suae necessitatis* and *necessarium per seipsum necessarium*. Only after drawing this distinction does he feel in a position to prove the existence of *aliquod primum necessarium quod est per seipsum necessarium*. And it is this, he says, which everybody calls 'God'.

The distinction between *necessaria* which have a cause and *necessaria* which have no cause is one to which Aquinas attached great importance. To prove the distinction he appeals, following Aristotle (*VIII Phys*, 252b2–5), to the case of geometrical proofs. It is a necessary truth that the three angles of a triangle equal two right angles; but the necessity of this truth has a cause, namely the necessity of the truth of the axioms from which it is deduced (*In VIII Phys*, 3; *In V Metaph*, 6).

Aquinas applied this distinction to the question, vexed among medieval Aristotelians, of the eternity of the heavenly bodies and the separate substances or angelic spirits. Just as some truths are always true, and yet their truth is caused: so, he explains, it is possible to believe that some beings have always existed and yet derive their existence from a cause. Therefore, though Aristotle may have believed the world to be eternal, he could yet regard God as the cause of the worlds's existence (*In VIII Phys*, 3). For *A* to be the cause of *B*'s existence, it is not necessary that it should be possible for *B* not to exist; it is sufficient that it should be the case that if *A* did not exist *B* would not exist – even though both the antecedent and the consequent of this proposition may be necessarily false (S. T. I, 44, 1 ad 2).

When he deploys this argument, Aquinas treats *necessarium* and its synonyms, and *perpetuum* and its synonyms, as equivalent to each other. (Compare together S. T. Ia 44, 1 ad 2; *In VIII Phys*, 3; *In VIII Phys*, 21; *In V Metaph*, 6.) He speaks as if whatever always exists cannot not exist. This is because he accepted the Aristotelian principle that what can happen sometimes does happen (S. T.Ia, 2, 3c etc.). Consequently, he would regard as a necessary being not only God but also any creature of God which had everlasting existence.

Are there, in fact, any such creatures? It is all very well for Aristotelians who believe in the eternity of the world to call the heavenly bodies *entia ex necessitate* – but what right has Aquinas, who believes that heaven and earth were created in time, to use the same phrase (S. T. Ia, 115, 6 ad 1)? Aquinas indeed believes that there is nothing contradictory in the notion of creation *ab aeterno*: he thinks that it is only by revelation from God that we know that the world had a beginning. But should he not conclude from this simply that the class of necessary beings *could have* had more than one member, though in fact it has only one?

In fact, Aquinas tells us quite explicitly in the *Summa contra Gentes* that some creatures are necessary beings. 'There are among created things' he writes 'some whose existence is necessary without any qualification or condition. For the existence of any being is necesary without any qualification or condition if that being has no possibility of not existing. Now some things have been brought into being by God in such a way that in their nature there is a power of not existing. That is because the matter in them is in potency to another form. Those things, therefore, in which there is no matter, or if there is, in which the matter is not in potency to another form, have no power of not existing. It may be said that things which come from nothing have a tendency, so far as in them lies, to return to nothing; and that therefore all creatures have a power of not existing. But this is manifestly a bad argument. It is said that created things tend to return to nothing in the same way as they come from nothing. But to say that they come from nothing is simply to refer to the power of the creator. There is not, therefore, in any created thing a power of not existing; but there is a power in the creator of choosing either to give them existence or to cease keeping them in existence.' (S. c. G. II, 30; Cf. *In VIII Phys*, 21)

The beings which Aquinas has in mind in this passage are the angelic spirits and the heavenly bodies. These, he believes, are incorruptible and indestructible by natural means: they can cease to exist only by being annihilated by God. His argument to prove that the possibility of being annihilated by God is not really a possibility of not existing seems a bad one. It is true that to say that God can make a planet out of nothing does not mean that there is something, called 'nothing', which has the possibility of being made by God into a planet; nor that there is a certain planet, which does not exist, but which has the power of being brought into existence by God. But it does not follow that when there *is* a planet, which does exist, and which God can annihilate, that the planet does not have the possibility of not existing.

Aquinas seems to have been misled here by excessive fidelity to Aristotle. He was similarly mistaken when in the Third Way he equated *'possibile esse et non esse'* to *'generabile vel corruptibile'*. In fact, he has defeated his own purpose. For a body which was created in time, even if *not* capable of annihilation, would not be a necessary substance in the Aristotelian sense. For what has not always existed is not an *ens perpetuum* and therefore not an *ens necessarium*.

In Aquinas' account there seems to be more than one mistake. But it would seem to be possible to avoid the strange consequences of his definitions of necessity in things and propositions in a very simple manner. If we were to treat the '*potest*' in '*quod non potest non esse*' as being not present, but tenseless, we would have a definition of '*necessarium*' which would work very well. It is because Aquinas treats the verb as significantly tensed that he regards a past-tensed proposition *in materia contingenti*, (which at one time *could* change its truth-value, but can now do so no longer) as a necessary proposition. It is for the same reason that he regards a substance which once did not exist, but which now exists incorruptibly, as a necessary substance.

If we amend Aquinas' definition, so that 'necessary' means 'what neither can, nor could, nor will be able not to be', then we can say that a necessary proposition is one which neither can nor could nor will be able to change its truth-value. This definition will not lead to the bizarre conclusions which we reached earlier. No proposition about a matter of history will be necessary by this definition; and no proposition will change in its lifetime from being contingent to being necessary or *vice versa*.

Even thus, however, we have not avoided the difficulty about the wholly indestructible substance which had a beginning. For though there was a time when such a substance *did not exist*, there was no time when it *could not exist*; for before it existed there was no such substance to have any capabilities at all. So we shall have to amend the definition further, and say that something is necessary if and only if it is, always will be, and always was; and cannot, nor could not, nor will be able not to be. With such a definition it seems to be possible to make sense of the medieval account of God as a necessary being, without being led into unacceptable conclusions.

5

The Argument from Design

One of the traditional forms of argument for the existence of God goes by the name 'the argument from design'. Perhaps the best-known presentation of the argument is the Fifth Way of the Five Ways of St Thomas Aquinas. The argument takes various forms: sometimes it is an argument based on an alleged cosmic order to be found in the universe; more commonly it is an argument from particular phenomena in the natural world where there is an appearance of the skilful adaptation of means to ends in contexts where no natural agent is visible who possesses the skill to plan the adaptation. Common to all versions of the argument is that one of the essential premises is the existence in nature of teleological phenomena.

G. H. von Wright, in his book *Explanation and Understanding* (London, 1968), drew a distinction between two traditions of scientific inquiry. One (which he called Aristotelian) could be regarded as teleological or finalistic; the other (which he called Galilean) could be regarded as causal or mechanistic. The latter has been broadly characteristic of the natural sciences, and has as its goal explanation; the latter has been characteristic of the historical sciences, or *Geistewissenschaften*, and has as its goal understanding. The paradigm of the explanatory procedure of the natural sciences has been the covering law model of explanation; the model of teleological intelligibility sought by the human sciences is the practical syllogism of Aristotle. As von Wright says: 'Broadly speaking, what the subsumption theoretic model is to causal explanation and explanation in the natural sciences, the practical syllogism is to teleological explanation and explanation in history and the social sciences.'

I think that von Wright's insight here is correct and profound. In the present paper I want to investigate whether it has application not in the area of the human sciences, where von Wright studied its impact, but at a more fundamental level. Clearly teleological explanation applies not only to the sciences of man: it is omnipresent, *prima facie* at least, in biology. The Nobel-prize-winning biologist Jacques Monod, in his *Chance and Necessity* (London, 1972), speaks of a 'fundamental characteristic common to all living beings without exception: that of being objects endowed with a purpose or project'. Do these two modes of intelligibility – explanation and understanding – apply not only at the superficial level to biology, but also at a more fundamental level? Do they apply at the most fundamental level of cosmic intelligibility? The argument from design seeks to show that they do: indeed that the level of understanding underlies the level of explanation.

Socrates, in Plato's *Phaedo*, describes his gradual disillusionment with the mechanistic explanations of natural science. He was pleased when he heard the Anaxagoras had explained everything by *nous* or mind; but he was disappointed by the total absence of reference to value in that philosopher's work. He was like someone who said that all Socrates' actions were performed with his intelligence, and then gave the reason why he was sitting here in prison by talking about the constitution of his body from bones and sinews, and the nature and properties of these parts, without mentioning that he judged it better to sit here in obedience to the Athenian court's sentence. 'If anyone wants to find out the reason why each thing comes to be or perishes or exists, this is what he must find out about it: how is it best for that thing to exist, or to act or be acted upon in any way?' (*Phaedo*, 97d). For Socrates, teleological explanation was deeper, more profound, than mechanistic explanation.

At the opposite extreme from Socrates stood Descartes. 'I consider the usual inquiries about final causes to be wholly useless in physics; it could not but be rash for me to investigate the aims of

God.' Gassendi objected that rejecting final causes meant rejecting the best argument for the existence of God. Descartes was unmoved: a study of the parts of plants and animals might make us praise their maker but would not tell us for what end he acted. The knowledge of a thing's purpose would never tell us its nature: the practice of arguing from ends was Aristotle's greatest fault. God's purposes are hidden from us and it is rash to want to plunge into them. (*Fourth Meditation*; *Fifth Replies*; *Entretien avec Burman*, n. 29). For Descartes it is mechanistic explanation, not teleological, which is fundamental for the philosopher of nature.

Contemporary scientific thought is more sympathetic to Descartes than to Socrates. Jacques Monod attributes to Descartes the discovery of the canon of scientific objectivity. 'The cornerstone of the scientific method is the postulate that nature is objective. In other words, the *systematic* denial that "true" knowledge can be reached by interpreting phenomena in terms of final causes – that is to say, of "purpose" ' (*Chance and Necessity*, p. 30). Modern mechanistic explanations of teleological phenomena are however less austerely mechanistic than Descartes himself would have wished. His aim was to explain all that happens in nature simply by the geometrical properties of matter in motion. The fundamental properties of matter called in aid in modern explanations of the behaviour of living beings go far beyond the sparse apparatus of Cartesian cosmology. But the explanations given are mechanistic in the sense of being explanations in terms of initial conditions and covering laws in whose statement no value-terms appear.

Descartes, it is well known, rejected explanation of gravity in terms of the attraction between bodies, on the grounds that this was a teleological explanation which postulated in inert bodies knowledge of a goal or terminus. But the essence of teleological explanation is not the fact that the explanation is given *ex post*, or by reference to the *terminus ad quem*. It is rather the part played in the explanation by the notion of purpose: the pursuit of good and the avoidance of evil. Nor is it essential to teleological explanation that it should be regular – or, for that matter, that it should be irregular. Newtonian inertia and Newtonian gravity provide examples of regularities which are not beneficial for the agents which exhibit them. All teleological explanation is in terms of the benefit of agents: but within this there are *ex ante* regularities (like instinctive avoidance behaviour) *ex post* regularities (like specific habits of nest-building); there are also *ex ante* explanations of non-rule governed behaviour (such as human action out of the motive of revenge) and *ex post* explanations of non-rule governed behaviour (such as the explanation of human action in terms of intention and purposes).

The nature of teleological explanation is often misstated both by its critics and by its defenders. Critics allege that to accept a teleological explanation is to accept backwards causation: the production of a cause by its effect. Whether or not backwards causation is the nonsense it is usually taken to be, teleological explanation does not involve any acceptance of it, as Charles Taylor showed. All that is necessary is that the law covering the behaviour of a teleological agent should be of the form '*A* will do whatever behaviour *B* is required in circumstances *C* to achieve its goal *G*'. What are the standard goals of an agent *A*, and what behaviour is required in particular circumstances may be subjects of straightforward empirical inquiry. Someone offering a teleological explanation is not saying that the goal is the efficient cause of the behaviour. On the contrary, the behaviour brings the goal into effect, if it is successful. If it is not successful, the goal never comes into being; if backwards causation was what was in question, we would here have an effect without its cause.

At the other extreme, defenders of teleological explanation have been known to claim that all causal explanation is somehow teleological. Causal laws, it is argued, if they are not to be subject to constant falsification in the real world, must be stated in terms of the tendency of causal agents to produce certain effects. But are not laws stated in terms of tendencies teleological laws, since tendencies are defined in terms of their upshot? Aquinas seems to have argued that since many actions of natural agents are described by verbs which import the bringing about of certain ends (as wetting is bringing it about that something is wet, and cooling is bringing it about that something is cool), all natural agents, and not just living ones, act for the sake of ends. But an act may be defined by its result, and a tendency be specified as a tendency to perform such an act, without this 'end' in the sense of final state being an 'end' in the sense of a goal. Not every result of an action is a goal of that action. A tendency is only teleological if it is a tendency to do something for the benefit (of the agent, or of something bearing a special relation to the agent).

In truth, teleological agency is neither universal (as Aquinas maintained) nor mythological (as some modern sceptics have argued). It is above all characteristic of living organisms. Monod says that endowment with a purpose is a fundamental characteristic of all living beings without exception: 'the latter are distinct from all other structures or systems present in the universe by this characteristic property, which we shall call teleonomy.'

Any teleological explanation must involve an activity which can be done well or badly, or an entity for which there can be good or bad. The paradigm of such entities is the living organism: that has needs, can flourish, can sicken, decay and die. Let us call entities for which there can be good and bad *beneficiaries*. Not only living beings are beneficiaries: so are their parts, artefacts, environments; for them too things can be good or bad. Thus beneficiaries include the organs of animals (eyes, liver, etc); artefacts, such as nests, vehicles, honeycombs, tools; and social institutions such as the family, legal punishment, armies. Numbers, classes, rocks, dust, mud are not beneficiaries: things are not good or bad for them. The theoretical entities of physics, likewise, are not beneficiaries.

Only beneficiaries can have purposes, though not all beneficiaries have purposes. All trees are beneficiaries, like other living things; but an individual tree, in the wild, does not have a purpose (though of course a tree may be planted in a garden for a purpose, such as to shade a particular corner; and if there is a God the existence of trees in general no doubt has its place in some overall plan). But only what has things good or bad for it can have a purpose, and the purposes of those things which are not living organisms are derived from the good or bad of organisms. A thing can have a purpose if it is a part of, or a context for, something which has a good of its own.

There are two ways in which things may have purpose: they may exist to serve a purpose, and they may act for a purpose. The first kind of purpose is function: things which exist for a purpose have that purpose as their function. Thus the organs of animals operate to serve a particular purpose which is their function: they are indeed defined by their function. Thus to describe something as a heart is to refer to the purpose it serves in an organism: that of pumping blood. The circulation of the blood is the function which not only defines the heart, but gives the reason for its existence: that is why animals have hearts, in order to circulate their blood.

The complex organisms within which the organs have their role or function do not themselves, in the same way, have functions. Some of them, such as plants, perhaps do not have purposes at all; however, animals have purposes, but not functions. That is to say, their existence does not in the normal case serve a purpose, but they perform many actions with a purpose: spiders weave webs, birds build nests, dogs dig up buried bones.

Having a purpose does not involve, necessarily, knowledge or intention of that purpose. Not all purposes of entities are conscious goals or projects of that entity. The activity of the spider has as its purpose the construction of the web, as the activity of the dog has as its purpose the retrieval of the bone; but the dog is conscious of the purpose of its activity as the spider is not. Not all purposeful actions are intentional actions, and not all entities with purposes are entities that have been designed by those whose needs they serve. Whether or not my liver was designed by God, it was certainly not designed by me.

Purpose, then, is not the same as design. The difference between the two is this. Design is purpose deriving from a conception of the good which fulfils the purpose. Both entities and actions may be designed, though the notion of design is more at home when we are speaking of entities and systems than when we are speaking of actions. When we are speaking of actions it is more naural to speak of them as intentional than to speak of them as designed. But just as purpose in the broad sense includes both the functions of entities and the goals of actions, so design, as purpose deriving from conception of the good, includes both the design of structures and the intentions with which agents act.

What is meant by saying that design is purpose deriving from a conception of the good? A conception of the good may be manifested in representations of it (as in the patterns, blueprints, descriptions and thoughts of human designers) or in expressions of it (as in the display of pleasure in animals). When purpose is design the design may either be immanent to the purposive agent (as with the projects of humans) or imposed from without (as with the function of artefacts).

It is beyond doubt that there are many phenomena in the world which can and should be explained teleologically: such and such happens in order to achieve such and such a purpose. But is such teleological explanation basic, or is it to be reduced to some other kind of explanation? Is the purpose in the world which is neither design immanent to the agent, nor imposed by any terrestrial designer, a basic fact of the world? Or is it something which must be explained by non-terrestrial design, or terrestrial non-purposive agents?

Socrates in the *Phaedo*, having compared mechanistic explanation to its disadvantage with teleological explanation, goes on to introduce what he regards as the safest kind of explanation of all: only by beauty are things beautiful, only by largeness are things large. In addition to mechanistic explanation and teleological explanation, we might say, he commends to us tautological explanation. Corresponding to the three Socratic types of explanation is the threefold Kantian classification of proofs of the existence of God. To tautological explanation corresponds the ontological argument; to mechanistic explanation, the cosmological argument; to teleological explanation, the physico-theological argument. The physico-theological argument, 'never to be mentioned without respect' is Kant's version of the argument from design. The argument is not nowadays popular, and I want to inquire whether there is anything to be said for it.

It has been pointed out more than once that the argument is ill-named. It is not the step from design to a designer that calls for complicated argument, or meets with much resistance; it is the step from purpose to design. The argument might best be called the argument through design: from purpose, through design, to a designer.

Common to both proponents and critics of the argument from design – nowadays at least – is the premise that naked purpose is inconceivable. That is, if we have an explanation in terms of purpose, that explanation cannot be a rock-bottom, basic-level explanation: it must be reducible either to an explanation in terms of design (intelligent purpose) or to an explanation in mechanistic terms. I shall not question this premise, but it might be questioned, and indeed would have been denied by philosophers as diverse as Aristotle and Bergson. The question, given this premise, is this. Which is the appropriate basic explanation of purpose: is it design, or chance, or necessity?

Let us start from the cases where our understanding is greatest: human artefacts. If I ask why the room in which I type is at 65 degrees the answer is that there is a thermostat set to preserve that temperature. That is a teleological explanation: an explanation of the thermostat's behaviour in terms of its function. But of course there is also a mechanistic explanation of how the thermostat works, say in terms of the expansion of metals (which, *pace* Aquinas, is not teleological). Which of these explanations is more basic? The mechanistic one is more basic in two senses. It operates upon principles of greater generality, which apply to many more things than this particular artefact; and it will explain not only the correct functioning but also the breakdown of the machinery. (If your thermostat breaks down, you send for a mechanic, not a teleologist.) On the other hand, if we ask for an explanation of how the machinery exists at all – which from another point of view is the more basic question – we must seek this once again in teleological terms: the purposes of the designer and manufacturer, and the needs of human beings for a particular environment.

With regard to the artefact, is this the ultimate level of explanation? The answer to be given to this will depend upon one's philosophical view of the explanation of human action. Someone who is a libertarian and an indeterminist will regard the decisions of the human beings involved in the construction of the thermostat as a terminus of explanation. A compatibilist, on the other hand, may have an open mind on the question whether these free decisions and actions may not be susceptible to explanation at a level of greater generality, in the way in which the operation of the thermostat was open to explanation which was, in that sense, more basic. A compatibilist who is also a determinist presumably goes further and believes that at a deeper level than the psychological one there is a mechanistic explanation of the decisions, in terms of some discipline either already existing or yet to be developed.

What of living organisms? Here there are many areas where teleology is involved. Leaving aside the special problems of consciousness and intelligence, there seem to be five principal points at which teleology operates and where teleology must be eliminated if there is to be hope of success in any reductionist programme to eliminate purposive explanation in favour of explanation in terms of non-purposive agents. First, there is the operation of mature living organisms; secondly there is the operation of the organs within those organisms. These two phenomena would call for explanation even if every organism came into existence in full maturity as Athena emerged from the head of Zeus. But in fact living individuals develop from embryonic states, and the morphogenesis of the individual is one of the most mysterious of teleonomic phenomena. Fourthly, on the assumption that not all the species now in existence have always been in existence, there is the problem of accounting for the emergence of new species; fifthly and finally, there is the question of the origin of speciation and life itself.

These are five levels at which purpose may seem to call for a designer. One who rejects both transcendent design and naked purpose must reduce the teleological elements here to mechanistic ones. Perhaps the evolution of life is the unfolding of an inevitable process, explained by the natural properties of non-living matter; perhaps it is the result of the operation of necessitating forces upon the outcome of chance occurrences. The latter seems to be the favoured option among contemporary biologists. In his book Monod speaks of 'Pure chance, absolutely free but blind, at the very root of the stupendous edifice of evolution: this central concept of modern biology is . . . the sole conceivable hypothesis'.

With regard to each of the levels of teleology we can raise both the questions: How does it work? Why does it exist? But it is clear that the answers to each of these questions at different levels may be related to each other. When we ask of the operation of an individual organ or its parts 'How does it work?' there may, or may not be, a mechanistic explanation in terms of, say, the stereospecific activities of proteins. In very many cases, no doubt, such an explanation will not be available; but it would be rash to claim that we know that there are some for which a mechanistic explanation is impossible. But even if at this level such an explanation were forthcoming for every teleological phenomenon there would remain the question: how does this system come to exist? The answer to this question, in the case of each individual, will be the story of its generation, its procreation. The procreative cycle is itself something whose existence cries out for explanation; but to explain it is to explain the existence of the species of which it is characteristic. It is thus that a reductive explanation of the existence of species hopes to provide a reductive explanation of the other teleological problems also. The properties of individual organisms, teleonomic as these are, are regarded as given to the individual by membership of a species; whatever the mechanism underlying the development or operation of the individual, the existence of the mechanism is to be explained by the individual's membership of the species; it is created in accordance with the blueprint the individual has inherited from its forebears. The origin of particular species, it is claimed, is explained by the mechanisms of evolutionary pressure and selection. But these mechanisms cannot be used to explain the origin of species as such: they cannot explain the existence of breeding populations, since that is one of the principles of evolutionary explanation. It is the origin of living, reproducing organisms which must be explained, by chance, necessity, or both, if we are to succeed with the reductionist programme.

What is it to explain something by chance? There are two kinds of chance which are explanatory factors. One is the chance which is the unsought outcome of the operation of one or more causes (where more than one cause is in play, this kind of chance is coincidence). The other kind of chance is the tendency of a cause to produce its proper effect n times out of m. The two kinds may be linked together in a particular case: a throw of a double six when dicing is an instance of both kinds of chance. Chance in the second sense is a genuine – if indeterministic – principle of explanation; chance in the first sense is the offshoot of a genuine principle of explanation. There is a third sense of chance – the *a priori* calculus of probability – which is not an explanatory principle at all; its function in relation to explanation is heuristic, to show where an explanation is needed and where none is needed.

Neither kind of explanatory chance necessarily rules out design.

A designer may put together two non-conspiring causes in such a way that the outcome is one not sought (pursued, tended towards) by either cause; he may include among the causes indeterministic ones (as a computer programmer may include a randomizing element in his program). But if the origin of life can be explained by the chance operation of the properties of non-living matter, then while there may be a designer or architect of the universe, there is no argument from design.

It has been argued by Dr M. Geach[1] that chance could never explain the emergence of a natural power. Chance may bring about an event or action which corresponds to the desription of the exercise of a power; but it could not produce it as the exercise of a power. The distinction between actions which are and are not exercises of power is, I believe, a genuine one. A horse may dam a river (by falling in accidentally); in doing so it is not exercising a power to dam rivers such as the power possessed by beavers.

Correspondingly, Geach argues, though a set of molecules might fortuitously come into a concatenation corresponding to that of a living organism, it could not fortuitously acquire the power of reproduction. For when we have a reproductive series of organisms, the procreation of each organism is an exercise of a single power, active from case to case. Whereas if the first organism had been the result of chance, then each successive organism in the generative series would be a further, coincidental chance. And this is incredible.

This argument, it seems to me, moves too fast. It is true that if something is F by chance, then it is not the result of the operation of a power to make F. The exercises of natural powers, even the first exercise of a natural power, cannot be something that happens by chance. But does it follow that a natural power could not be acquired by chance?

It seems clear that natural powers can be conferred by art. The powers of man-made fibres appear to be natural powers, even though they are powers of artefacts. (At least they do not seem to be artificial powers in the way that a clock's power to tell the time is an

1 In an unpublished doctoral dissertation, submitted to Cambridge University.

artificial power.) But if art can confer a natural power, why cannot chance? As Aristotle observed, art and chance work in the same field.

We may distinguish between powers and their vehicles. The vehicle of a power is the substance or structure in virtue of which an agent possesses a power (as a round peg has the power of fitting into a round hole in virtue of being round, and whisky has the capacity to intoxicate in virtue of containing alcohol). In so far as a power arises from its vehicle, then chance can confer a power. For certainly chance could cause a certain shape or structure (such as being round); in so far as it did so, it would confer the power (e.g. of fitting into a round hole).

If something acquires a natural power by chance, it gets it not through the operation of any natural power: there is no natural or artificial agent whose operation is the production of that power. Is this paradoxical? Is there anything repugnant in the idea that by chance a certain structure is produced and that structure confers a certain power, contingently by the operation of nature?

There is nothing paradoxical here, because there are two different things in question. What is by chance and not by nature, is that such and such a structure comes into being. What is by nature and not by chance is that such and such a structure has such and such powers. The chance event must of course itself be the product of natural powers; but why may not the powers which produce the event be conditional rather than absolute powers: powers to ϕ under certain conditions, rather than absolutely. Thus, for instance, a certain structure may result by chance in the sense that there is no agent which has, absolutely, the power to produce that structure. Thus a certain megamolecule results though there is no molecule which has a power to produce such a structure; but perhaps two molecules each have conditional powers, which are exercised only if they meet another molecule of the appropriate kind, and thus the structure results by the chance which is the coincident operation of non-conspiring causes.

It is not clear to me that it is in any stronger sense than this that the customary story of the origin of life from the primeval soup demands that chance explains the origin of natural powers. Of course the powers that are to be explained if we want to explain the origin of life are powers of a special kind: not just the power to make things *F* but the power to make things have a power to make things *F*; what we might call replicative powers. But these do not appear to present special difficulties once we have admitted that natural powers of any kind can be produced by chance.

I confess, however, to feeling residual hesitations about the accounts of the origin of life which I have seen. The difficulties perhaps arise from the popular nature of the expositions which I have read, or betray my own misunderstanding. But it is a common feature of all the accounts which I have read that they fail to make simultaneously plausible two elements which must both be explained if we are to account for the origin of life from the random motion of non-living molecules. To the extent that the random formation of groupings is made plausible, to explain the emergence of the first living cells, to the same extent the account makes less credible the origin of like from like alone which is the essence of reproduction by breeding. I must leave it to others to decide whether this is a contingent or necessary feature of popular accounts of the biological theory of the origin of life.

What, then, shall we say of the argument from design? The argument in its simplest form goes as follows:

1 Wherever there is purpose there is a designer.
2 There is purpose which has no designer in the natural world.
3 Therefore, there is a designer outside the natural world.

The second premise is undeniably true. The first premise is not a tautology, given the definitions I have offered of purpose and design: purpose is identified quite differently from design, purpose by identifying the regular goal-directed behaviour, design by locating the conception of the good from which it arises. But is it true?

One reason for thinking it true might be that one had reason to believe that there is a God who is the creator of the universe. But this is a reason which clearly cannot be offered by someone who is offering the argument from design not just as a valid argument but as a proof which might lead someone from ignorance of God to knowledge of God. What other reasons are there for thinking it to be true? What reasons are there for thinking it false?

The strongest reason for thinking it false is that it seems clear that there can be purpose without a designer if the purpose can be given a mechanistic explanation, so that it is reducible to the operation of necessity and chance. To take account of this, it is necessary to restate the premisses of the argument from design thus:

1a Wherever there is irreducible purpose there is a designer.
2a There is irreducible purpose which has no designer in the natural world.

In this formulation the first premise gains much greater plausibility: but, by contrast, the second premise is now no longer undeniably true.

I am strongly inclined to believe that 1a is in fact true, for the following reason. Though teleological phenomena do not imply backwards causation, they do none the less present a problem analogously related to the temporal sequence. It is essential to teleological explanation that it should be in terms of a good to be achieved; yet the good which features in the explanation, at the time of the event to be explained, does not yet exist and indeed may never exist. This is difficult to understand except in the case where the good pre-exists in the conception of the designer: the mind of the designer exists at the appropriate time, even if the good designed does not. It is for this reason that most modern thinkers – atheistic as well as theistic – deny that there can be any such thing as naked purpose. But the authority of Aristotle may make us hesitate before claiming 1a as a self-evident truth.

In the course of the paper I have considered the reasons which might be given for believing 2a to be true. The reader may have been surprised that I have had very little to say about natural selection. That is principally because I believe that the main philosophical elements of the argument from design – though not the examples that might be cited of teleology – remain, for better or worse, much the same before and after Darwinism. But in conclusion I should spell out the way in which the possibility of explanation by natural selection does effect the consideration of teleological phenomena.

In a Darwinian explanation we offer to explain the following fact

1   Members of species S' have feature F for the sake of advantage G.
    by the following sequence.
2   Members of earlier species S sometimes have F and sometimes do not have F.
3   Members of S which have F have advantage G.
4   Members of S without F did not breed successfully.
5   Only members of S with F survived, so now all S's have F.

A Darwinian explanation has it in common with teleological explanation that notions of good and evil ('advantage') figure esentially in it. But unlike teleological explanation, Darwinian explanation contains the reference to the good at a point in the explanation when the phenomenon to be explained is still in the future. To the extent that it is successful, therefore, a Darwinian explanation removes the surd in pure purpose which seemed to cry out for a designer. But the extent of Darwinian explanation is limited by its form. As remarked earlier, it may explain the origin of particular species, but it cannot explain the origin of Species as such. This becomes clear from the pattern above. If one uses as the substitution instance of F 'the power to breed' then proposition 4 does indeed come out true: but the explanatory ring has somehow gone out of the sequence.

The major difficulty with the argument from design, therefore, is the difficulty of reaching a decision about the truth-value of premise 2a. But it is worth remarking, and has often been remarked before, that even if successful the argument from design seems to fall short of establishing the existence of the creator of Judaeo-Christian tradition. Since design is adaptation of natural powers, the question of the origin of natural powers is irrelevant to the argument from design as such, unless the powers are powers to perform teleological activities. (It may have been because Aquinas regarded all natural powers as teleological that he could conclude the Fifth Way by saying 'and this all men call God'.) Kant was right to say that the physico-theological argument leads to a designer, or architect, not a creator of the universe. Moreover, even if the phenomena of purpose do clamour for design as their explanation, it takes further argument to show that what we have to do with here is a single designer, rather than a harmonious group of ingenious spirits.

More serious still, supposing that the proposed explanations by chance and necessity are inadequate, what is added to the recognition of its inadequacy by attributing purpose to design? Descartes was wrong to say that any appeal to final causes involves a claim to know God's arcane designs. On the contrary, when we recognize a teleological phenomenon, we know very well what the purpose is, otherwise we would not have seen the phenomenon as tending to a *telos*. The question is not what the purpose is, but whose it is. Of course, if God has an overarching purpose in creating the universe, this is not discovered when we decide that it is his design which enables the eye to focus or the liver to perform its function. But one can offer the argument from design without claiming to do that, and *a fortiori* one can give teleological explanations of natural phenomena without making any such claim.

The difficulty is rather in giving content to the notion of a supernatural mind. Earlier, I said that design was purpose deriving from a conception of the good; and I could illustrate what a conception of the good was by its representation in the case of human beings, and its expression in the case of animals. No similar manifestation of the conception of the good seems to be appropriate in the case of a non-bodily, supernatural, transcendent designer. The conclusion of the argument from design can only be made intelligible if there is some independent account to be given of the coherence of transcendent mind.

It is sometimes said that the argument from design leads to a 'God of the gaps': a God invoked merely to fill the gaps left by scientific explanation at any given point in history. If the argument from design is to succeed, the God it points to must be a God of necessary gaps, that is to say, gaps in explanation which can be demonstrated not to be capable of being filled by a particular type of explanation (as, I have claimed, Darwinian explanation cannot explain the origin of true-breeding species). If the argument is to succeed, only necessary gaps in explanation can be invoked: the God of contingent gaps would have only a precarious hold on worship.

6

Mystical Experience:
St John of the Cross

Mysticism and poetry are often contrasted with philosophy and reasoning; and mystics have sometimes despised philosophy. Not so St John of the Cross. He studied philosophy for three years – from 1564 to 1567 – at the University of Salamanca, then a renowned centre of scholastic learning; and when later he wrote his spiritual treatises, he took great pains to expound his mystical theology within the framework of the scholastic categories. His works are thus of almost unique interest for the philosophy of religion, combining as they do the attributes of mystical and philosophical writing.

St John is best known, of course, not as a philosopher but as a poet. His life's work of reforming, with St Teresa of Avila, the Carmelite order in Spain drew upon him the hostility of the unreformed Carmelites; in 1577 he was kidnapped and imprisoned by these friars in the priory at Toledo. While in prison he wrote a number of verses, of which the most famous are the *Spiritual Canticle* and *Dark Night*. These very beautiful stanzas appear, on first reading, to be straightforward love poems written in the person of the woman; and to this day in some quarters the poems are read and enjoyed as such. But they are obviously derivative from the Song of Songs and *Dark Night* bears the title 'Songs of the soul in rapture at having arrived at the height of perfection, which is union with God by the road of spiritual negation'. The poems were circulated, as devotional works, among the friars and nuns of the

Carmelite reform. St John was pressed to write commentaries on them, and it was thus that his mystical treatises came into being. He left four main prose works, all written as commentaries on his poems: the *Spiritual Canticle*, and the *Living Flame of Love*, commentaries on the poems of the same names; and *Ascent of Mount Carmel* and *Dark Night of the Soul*, which are not really separate works, but two incomplete parts of a single commentary projected on the poem *Dark Night*. The poem is a very brief one – eight five-line stanzas – and only the first two stanzas were commented upon by St John in his lifetime; but these fragmentary commentaries take up between them 450 pages of the English edition. Together they make up St John's most systematic exposition of his mystical theology.[1]

In this paper I shall try to do two things. First I shall try to set out the main lines of St John's mystical theology, so far as possible in his own words; then I shall propose for discussion some problems in the understanding of it which are suggested by contemporary philosophical interests.

The Dark Night of the Sense, St John says, 'pertains to beginners'. He is thinking primarily of Carmelites: the description he gives of beginners makes clear that, by worldly standards, they are already exceptionally devout. They find their delights, he says, in spending whole nights in prayer, they make penances and fasts their joys, and they find their consolation in the sacraments and the thoughts of divine things. Such people are, however, imperfect in a many ways: they tend to be proud of their austerities, to be censorious and stubborn, and to be childishly attached to particular forms and accessories of devotion. To cure them of these imperfections God puts them into the dark night of sense. (I, 331)

The dark night of the sense consists in the deprivation of the appetite of the soul of all pleasures of sight, sound, smell, taste and touch. It is impossible, of course, to go through life without using the five senses, or without encountering pleasant sights and tastes and sensations; but the soul must strive to free itself from all attachments to the objects of the senses. (II, 22) It must strip itself

1 References are given to the English translation of St John's works by E. Allison Peers (London, 1953).

of any desire for, or pleasure in, any creature. This is because creatures and God are two contraries which cannot co-exist in the soul together. Since there is nothing that equals God, the soul that loves some other thing together with him, or clings to it, does him a grievous wrong.

'All the being of creation compared with the infinite Being of God is nothing. And therefore the soul that sets its affection upon the being of creation is likewise nothing in the eyes of God, and less than nothing; for love makes equality and similitude and even sets the lover below the object of his love. And therefore such a soul will in no wise be able to attain to union with the infinite being of God; for that which is not can have no communion with that which is.' (*Asc.* I, 25). The beauty, wisdom, liberty and delight of the world is ugliness, foolishness, slavery and misery in the sight of God.

Remembering the command to love our neighbour as well as to love God, we may well wonder whether St John means that *all* desires for creatures are to be banished from the soul, or only sinful ones, i.e. ones in contravention of divine law. St John's answer is clear enough. There are natural desires which we cannot help having; but so far as we can, all voluntary desires are to be rooted out. Only a voluntary desire for something mortally sinful wholly cuts us off from God; but a single unruly desire, although there be in it no matter of mortal sin, suffices to bring a soul into such bondage, foulness and vileness that it can in no wise come to accord with God in union until the desire be purified. Any desire, though it be but for the smallest imperfection, stains and defiles the soul. These habitual imperfections are, for example, a common custom of much speaking, or some slight attachment which we never wish to conquer, such as that to a person, a garment, a book, a particular kind of food, tittle tattle, fancies for tasting, knowing and hearing certain things, and such like (I, 43–9).[2] As long as the soul is attached to anything there is no possibility that it will make progress to perfection, even though the imperfection be extremely slight. For it comes to the same thing whether a bird be held by a slender cord or by a stout one; even if it be slender, the bird will be

---

2 Cf. I, 245 on not rejoicing in worldly goods – including wife, children, etc.

as well held as if it were stout, so long as it breaks it not and flies not away. (I, 44–6)

St John ends the first part of his treatise by giving rules for those who would enter into the night of sense. Let them first try to behave in all things as Christ would behave, meditating on his life so that they may know how to imitate him. Secondly, every pleasure which presents itself to the the senses, if it be not purely for the honour and for the glory of God, must be renounced and completely rejected for the love of Jesus Christ.

When the external senses have been perfected in this manner, St John tells us, by mortifying the palate at meals and chastening the sense of touch by penance and holy rigour, God is wont to perfect them still further;

> by bestowing on them certain supernatural favours and gifts, in order to confirm them the more completely in that which is good, offering them certain supernatural communications, such as visions of saints or holy things in corporeal shape, the sweetest perfumes, locutions, and exceeding great delights of touch, wherewith sense is greatly confirmed in virtue and is withdrawn from a desire for evil things. And besides this He continues at the same time to perfect the interior bodily senses, such as imagination and fancy, and to habituate them to that which is good, by means of considerations, meditations and reflections of a sacred kind, in all of which he is instructing the spirit. And when these are prepared by this natural exercise, God is want to enlighten and spiritualize them still more by means of certain supernatural visions. (I, 131)

While still at a comparatively early stage of its progress, then, the soul may expect to receive visions in the external and internal senses (I, 95). St John does not explain exactly what is the difference between the two sorts of visions. It is apparently not the same as the difference between public and private visions, since the Transfiguration, which was seen by three apostles together, is described as a vision in the interior senses. But St John distinguishes many different types of supernatural visitation which the soul may receive. Besides seeing visions strictly so called, a man may hear supernatural sounds or smell spiritual fragrances or feel super- naturally delicious sensations. Or he may receive messages from God or come to know truths by other than natural means, or have mysteries revealed to him, or see spiritual visions, like Jesus' vision of all the kingdoms of the world, which could not all be seen at once with the bodily eye. St John devotes many pages to describing such manifestations, and suggesting how they may be distinguished and classified. But his constant advice to the soul which receives such experiences is to take no notice of them. Visions and voices can be produced by the devil as well as by God; messages even from God can be misunderstood; extraordinary experiences generate pride and dissipate the mind (I, 229). It is too much of a waste of time to try to sort out good visions from bad: reject them all and think no more about them. If, after all, they come from God, they will do the soul good whether the soul accepts them or not. It is a sin to desire to know things by supernatural means. 'Such great use' he says, 'must we make of our reason and of Gospel doctrine that if certain things be told us supernaturally ... we must receive only that which is in clear conformity with reason and Gospel law. And then we must receive it, not because it is revelation, but because it is reason.' (I, 155)

It is common to think of mystics as people who have certain special experiences. St John of the Cross never uses the phrase 'mystical experience' – where the word 'experience' appears in the English it is an importation of the translator – and when he does speak of extraordinary experiences it is always with suspicion.[3] His constant teaching is that no human activity which had the characteristics of an experience could have God for its object. 'All distinct images and kinds of knowledge both natural and super- natural, that can be encompassed by the faculties of the soul, however lofty they be in this life, have no comparison or proportion with the Being of God' (I, 233). God is in no genus, and the soul in this life has not the capacity to receive clearly and distinctly anything which does not fall under genus and species. 'All that can be understood by the understanding, that can be tasted by the will,

3 Cf. I, 72, 131, 134, 140ff., 155.

and that can be invented by the imagination is most unlike to God and bears no proportion to him.'

As an example of St John's rather high-handed way with Scripture, we may quote a passage in which he claims to detect this doctrine in Isaiah.

> All this Isaiah admirably explained in that most noteworthy passage where he says 'To what thing have ye been able to liken God? Or what image will ye make that is like to Him? Will the workman in iron perchance be able to make a graven image? Or will he that works gold be able to imitate Him with gold, or the silversmith with plates of silver?' By the workman in iron is signified the understanding, the office of which is to form intelligences and strip them of the iron of species and images. By the workman in gold is understood the will, which is able to receive the figure and the form of pleasure, caused by the gold of love. By the silversmith, who is spoken of as being unable to form Him with plates of silver, is understood the memory, with the imagination, whereof it may be said with great propriety that its knowledge and the imaginings that it can invent and make are like plates of silver. And thus it is as though he had said: Neither the understanding with its intelligence will be able to understand aught that is like Him, nor can the will taste pleasure and sweetness that bears any resemblance to that which is God, neither can the memory set in the imagination ideas and images that represent Him. (I, 92)

It is in order to purify a man from the distracting contents of the imagination, the understanding and the will that God sets him in the second and more terrible night, the dark night of the spirit. Paradoxically, this night is also called the illuminative way. St John explains:

> When the light of God illumines man, who is impure and weak, it plunges him into darkness and causes him affliction and distress, as does the sun to the eye that is weak; it enkindles him with passionate yet painful love, until he be

spiritualized and refined by this same fire and love . . . he receives this contemplation and loving knowledge in the constraint and yearning of love . . .

This enkindling and yearning of love is not always perceived by the soul. For in the beginning, when this spiritual purgation commences, all this divine fire is used in drying up and making ready the wood (which is the soul) rather than in giving it heat. But as time goes on, the fire begins to give heat to the soul, and the soul then very commonly feels this enkindling and heat of love. Further, as the understanding is being more and more purged by means of this darkness, it sometimes comes to pass that this mystical and loving theology, as well as enkindling the will, strikes and illuminates the understanding also. This enkindling of love, which accompanies the union of these two faculties . . . is for the soul a thing of great richness and delight: for it is a certain touch of the divinity and the beginning of the perfection of the union of love for which it hopes. (I, 411)

The dark night of the spirit begins when the soul finds itself no longer capable of meditation. Aridity in prayer may come, of course, from many sources, physiological or psychological; but there are three signs by which one may tell that the aridity is a sign from God that he is leading the soul to contemplation.

1   If the soul finds no pleasure in thinking of things other than God.
2   If it feels anxiety about not serving God.
3   If the 'soul takes pleasure in being alone and waits with loving attentiveness on God, without making any particular meditation, in inward peace annd quietness and rest, and without acts and exercises of the faculties – memory, understanding and will – at least, without discursive acts, that is without passing from one thing to another'. (I, 109)

The dark night of mystical contemplation is a time – lasting perhaps for years – of great suffering. For the first thing the soul perceives in the divine illumination is its own misery. The greatest suffering is the thought of abandonment by God. 'The soul in this purgation is conscious that it has a great love for God . . . yet this is no relief to it, but rather brings it greater affliction. For it loves Him so much that it cares about naught beside; when therefore it sees itself to be so wretched that it cannot believe that God loves it . . . it is grieved' (I, 393). It is unable to raise its affections or its mind to God, and nothing which its spiritual director says can comfort it. 'For the soul is so greatly absorbed and immersed in the realization of those evils wherein it sees its own miseries so clearly, that it thinks that, as its director observes not that which it sees and feels, he is speaking in this manner because he understands it not.' During this time a man may forget what he has been doing or where he is. (I, 125, 390–4)

> In the midst of these times of aridity and hardship God communicates to the soul, when it is least expecting it, the purest spiritual sweetness and love, together with a spiritual knowledge which is sometimes very delicate, each manifestation of which is of greater benefit and worth than those which the soul enjoyed aforetime; although in the beginnings the soul thinks that this is not so; for the spiritual influence now granted to it is very delicate and cannot be perceived by sense. (I, 369)

So, after years of contemplation the dark night begins to give way to the dawn of union with God, whose full day will appear only in the beatific vision in the after life. St John describes the final stage of union lyrically under the metaphor of a mystical marriage; but it is difficult to find passages in which he attempts to describe the state without metaphor. Here are two of the least metaphorical passages.

> The supernatural union comes to pass when the two wills, of the soul and of God, are confounded together in one, and there is nought in one that is repugnant to the other. (I, 72ff.)

The second passage comes from a context in which St John is describing different revelations: all are to be rejected save one, which he calls 'knowledge of naked truths' (*inteligencia de verdades desnudas*). This is pure contemplation, which was experienced by David and Moses; the soul which does this 'sees clearly that there is no way wherein it can say aught concerning it . . . although at times when such knowledge is given to a soul, words are used, the soul is well aware that it has expressed no part of what it has felt; for it knows that there is no fit name by which it can name it'. These lofty manifestations of God do not concern particulars, and cannot be counterfeited by the devil, because they *are* union with God, and to receive them is equivalent to 'a certain contact with the divinity which the soul experiences' (*cierto toque che se nace del alma a la divinidad*) and thus it is God himself who is perceived and tasted therein. (I, 18)

> The road to God [St John summarizes] consists not in a multiplicity of meditations . . . nor in consolations . . . but only in the one thing that is needful, which is the ability to deny oneself truly, according to that which is without and to that which is within, giving oneself up to suffering for Christ's sake and to total annihilation. (I, 86)

So far I have merely expounded St John's teaching, to a great extent in his own words. The passages I have quoted do not give a fair impression of his style, for I have deliberately avoided metaphorical passages so far as possible. St John is a master of metaphor, and much of the incantational power of his writing comes from the skill with which, like a metaphysical poet, he can turn images from every field. But St John's very skill as a poet traps him often into giving metaphor in place of explanation. And it is this which gives rise to the problems which I want to discuss.

The reader's first difficulty with St John's writing is not in making sense of his account of the supernatural workings of the soul, but about its natural workings. It is possible to collect from his writings quite a detailed philosophy of mind, or anthropology.

Exterior senses: sight, smell, hearing, taste, touch
Interior senses: fancy
                   imagination[4]

4 On the relation between these see I, 72, 95.

Spirit: memory
                     understanding
                     will: capacity for joy, hope, grief, fear
Substance: locus of union with God.

This mental anatomy differs significantly from that of Aquinas. For
Aquinas the passions are not exercises of the will; and the memory
is an inner sense like the imagination, not a part of the spiritual soul
like the intellect. St John's account is in some ways closer to that of
Locke, and indeed, with regard to the natural workings of the
mind, he is a thoroughgoing empiricist. 'The understanding', he
says, in this life 'can understand nought save . . . forms and
imaginings of things that are received through the bodily senses.' It
is for this reason that nothing that the imagination can imagine or
the understanding receive can be a proximate means of union with
God (I, 90).

We can find in him many of the characteristic empiricist
doctrines – the comparison of the soul to a *tabula rasa* or a prisoner
seeing through windows (I, 22), the observation that the imagination can combine forms into, for example, a golden mountain, but
not make new forms (I, 95); the illustration of the man born blind
trying to imagine colours (I, 68). For St John sense-impressions
leave behind species, as for Hume impressions leave behind ideas
(I, 90). The intellect, for St John as for the empiricists, is not
creative; Aquinas' doctrine of the *intellectus agens* is here worn away
out of recognition; the function of the intellect is merely to recall
sense-impressions in their absence. St John accepts the empiricist
thesis that to experience *x* is a sufficient and necessary condition for
understanding *x* and for learning the meaning of the word '*x*': this
he expressly applies to mystical states – only he who has passed this
way can understand it (I, 1, 238). For St John as for Locke it is the
function of the inner sense to observe the acts of the mind. For St
John as for Locke the substance of a thing is an imperceptible
substrate: the faculties of the soul, he tells us, cannot, of their own
power reflect and act save upon some form, figure and image, and
this is the rind and accident of the substance and spirit which lies
beneath this rind and accident (I, 236). These close parallels with
Locke set an interesting problem for historians of philosophy.

Certainly there was no direct connection; it seems likely that both writers were drawing on a common background of decadent scholasticism.

A more startling, though more easily accountable, parallel may be made between St John and Descartes. St John's reasons why we should enter upon the dark night resemble Descartes' reasons for methodical doubt. The soul, says St John, must darken its memory:

It is clear that the soul must of necessity fall into many falsehoods, when it admits knowledge and reasoning: for oftentimes that which is true must appear false, and that which is certain doubtful; and contrariwise; or there is scarcely a single truth of which we can have complete knowledge. From all these things the soul is free if the memory enters into darkness with respect to every kind of reflection and knowledge.

Even the *génie malin* appears: St John tells us that the devil implants impressions in the fancy in such wise that those that are false appear true, and those that are true, false. St John's answer to the doubts which surround the soul is not the *cogito*, but a *non cogito*: a refusal to think at all. But if we are not to think at all, how can we think of God? St John answers, that Christ, who entered the upper room through closed doors, will enter spiritually into the soul, without the soul's knowing how he does so, when the doors of its faculties, memory understanding and will are enclosed against all apprehensions. (I, 219–21).

There are many tiny resemblances to Descartes – for instance the frequent use of the phrase 'clear and distinct' as a technical expression (e.g. I, 233). Here the historical connection is not far to seek. Many of the earliest Jesuits were trained at Salamanca, where St John learnt his philosophy; and Descartes owed his schooling to the Jesuits of la Flèche.

Among the difficulties which arise from St John's philosophy of mind, I will mention only three.

1   The empiricist account of the intellect which St John adopts has been shown in our own time to be fundamentally inadequate.

When St John tells us about the extraordinary operations of the soul in mystical states he does so by contrast with its ordinary operations. But he misdescribes the ordinary operations so radically that the contrasts he draws are unhelpful. When he tells us that the soul in a mystical state does not work as the soul is said to work by empiricist philosophers, I want to reply that when I know my own name or know how to tie my bootlaces, my soul does not work in the way that empiricist philosophers say that it does.

2   In particular, the concept of the inner senses is incoherent. The concept of *sense* seems to involve two things (a) that it should be a mode of acquiring knowledge to which the position of the body is relevant, and (b) that it should be possible for someone possessing a sense to be mistaken about its objects and to have his mistakes corrected by others. By the second of these criteria the memory, but not the imagination, might be allowed to be a sense; but the first criterion rules out both memory and imagination and the ability to give an account of one's own mental activities. The incoherence of this notion comes out constantly in the difficulty which St John has in deciding to which sense to attribute a particular type of supernatural experience.

3   The faculties of the soul get personified by St John, so that the intellect desires, and the will perceives, and is led captive (I, 393, 413). The use of faculty-language does not necessarily lead to philosophical incoherence. It is impossible altogether to avoid speaking of the will as the locus of desires and the intellect as the locus of knowledge. But it is important to be on one's guard against attributing to these loci properties which belong only to complete substances, the persons aspects of whose behaviour and abilities such notions as 'the intellect' and 'the will' systematize. There is a particular difficulty about the will in St John, which sometimes appears as the capacity for taking voluntary action, and sometimes as the locus of certain feelings, notably the passions of joy, grief, hope and fear (I, 72, 242). Above all, there is danger in speaking as St John does of the substance of the soul, as being a specially inaccessible part of the soul. We cannot avoid the impression in reading his account

of the final union that it is in the Lockean substratum that the contact with God ultimately takes place.[5]

It may be said that all these deficiencies belong only to the historical envelope in which St John's mystical teaching is wrapped. Can we make sense of what he says in its own right?

The characteristic of contemplation which St John most stresses is its secrecy:

> Contemplation is secret and hidden from the very person that experiences it; and ordinarily, together with the aridity and emptiness which it causes in the senses, it gives the soul an inclination and desire to be alone and in quietness, without being able to think of any particular thing or having the desire to do so. If those souls to whom this comes to pass knew how to be quiet at this time, and troubled not about performing any kind of action, whether inward or outward, neither had any anxiety about doing anything, then they would delicately experience this inward refreshment in that ease and freedom from care . . . It is like the air which, if one would close one's hand on it, escapes. (I, 354)

The soul, even when illumined, cannot speak of contemplation or give it a name whereby it may be called.

> For apart from the fact that the soul has no desire to speak of it, it can find no suitable way or manner or similitude by which it may be able to describe such lofty understanding and such delicate spiritual feeling . . . It is like one who sees something never seen before, whereof he has not even seen the like; although he might understand its nature and have experience of it, he would be unable to give it a name, or say what it is, however much he tried to do so. (I, 429)

A person contemplating can only say that he is satisfied, tranquil, and contented, and that he is conscious of the

5 Yet St John is not unaware of the dangers of faculty-psychology: see III, 110.

presence of God, and that, as it seems to him, all is going well with him; but he canot describe the state of his soul, nor can he say anything about it save in general terms like these. (I, 30)

In these pasages, it seems to me, St John has step by step deprived contemplation of all of the characteristics which make it possible to attribute to a person a spiritual activity. Most obviously, there is no bodily behaviour characteristic of contemplation: St John consistently rejects the suggestion that trances, levitation, trembling, etc., have any essential connection with the activities he is describing. Secondly, there is no possibility of expressing the activity of contemplation in words. But verbal and non-verbal expressions are the two criteria by which we attribute inner activities to people other than ourselves. But might not the mystic, as he says, perform an activity which he cannot communicate? We may first observe that if the mystic really cannot communicate the nature of his activity, then no mystic can have grounds for thinking that any other mystic is engaged on the same activity; St John has no right to say that David and Moses went in for contemplation (I, 193). But let this pass: if the mystic's activity is completely incommunicable, then at best the only, the decisive, criterion for the mystic's being engaged in this activity is his own word that he is doing so. But St John constantly insists that this is inadequate: from the passages quoted above it is clear both that a person may think he is contemplating when he is not, and may be contemplating without knowing it. True, we are offered some criterion whereby we can check the mystic's word: the effects of the contemplation on the mystic's life – tranquillity and virtue. There are passages where it appears that neither tranquillity nor great virtue are necessary accompaniments of genuine contemplation. Perhaps these passages can be satisfactorily explained: but even so, a difficulty remains. A contemplative, St John says, may think that in the time of prayer he is doing absolutely nothing (I, 108, 115, 354, 369, 429). How can we show that he is wrong? By pointing, St John says, to the good effects of his prayer. But unless we have some *other* criterion of what contemplating is, what right have we to speak of *effects* here at all? We have *A*, who prays in the ordinary way, and is only moderately tranquil and virtuous; we have *B*, who thinks he is saying no prayers at all, and is highly tranquil and virtuous. Why must we say: *B* must be contemplating, unknown to himself? Why may we not say: how mysterious are God's ways: he gives *A* only moderate virtue, though *A* says many prayers; and he gives *B* great virtue, though *B* says no prayers at all! So far as I can see, St John gives us no reason for describing *B*'s situation in one way rather than the other; and unless and until we are given some such reason, it seems possible to maintain that, when *B* thinks he is doing nothing in church, *B* may be absolutely right.

III

Grace, Freedom and Necessity

7

Grace and Freedom in
St John Chrysostom

St John Chrysostom never composed a theological treatise on grace after the manner of a Suarez or even an Augustine. He was a preacher rather than a theologian, and his doctrine is to be found scattered in innumerable places in his sermons. His teaching on grace is worth special investigation, because in various ways it seems to differ from the doctrine which became received in the Church after Augustine and the Council of Orange. Pelagius himself quoted St John's writings to support his denial of original sin. Augustine refuted Pelagius, showing that he had distorted Chrysostom's meaning. But there is more serious ground for asking whether Chrysostom can be considered as a precursor of the doctrine of the Massilienses or semi-Pelagians. This appears clearly in the notorious text from Chrysostom's homily on St Paul's words, 'habentes eundem spiritum fidei'. Chrysostom there asks why St Paul speaks not simply of 'faith' but of 'the spirit of faith'; and why he considers faith as a gift. He writes as follows:

> But why does he call it the *spirit* of faith, and include it in a list of the charismata? Because if faith is some sort of charisma – a gift of the spirit alone, and not an achievement of ours – then unbelievers will not be punished, nor will believers merit praise . . . A gift is not an achievement of the person who receives it, but a product of the generosity of the giver . . . Why then does he call it the spirit of faith? He wants to show

that the beginning of belief comes from our good will, and from our obedience to the call; but after the foundation of faith has been laid, then we need the help of the spirit, if faith is to remain in us unshakeable and unassailable. For neither God, nor the grace of the spirit precedes our own resolution. Though he calls us, he waits for us to approach him spontaneously and of our own will. Only then, when we have approached, does he confer all his help on us. (Migne, *Patrologia Graeca* – henceforth referred to as *P. G.* – Paris, 1807–66, Vol. 51, p. 276).

So Chrysostom. The Council of Orange, on the other hand, defined as follows:

Si quis sine gratia Dei credentibus, volentibus, desiderantibus . . . nobis misericordiam dicit conferri divinitus, non autem ut credamus, velimus, vel haec omnia sicut oportet agere valeamus, per infusionem Sancti Spiritus in nobis fieri confitetur; et aut humilitati, aut obedientiae humanae subjungit gratiae adiutorium, nec, ut obedientes et humiles simus, ipsius gratiae donum esse consentit, resistit Apostolo dicenti: 'Quid habes quod non accepisti?'. (Denzinger-Bannwart, *Enchiridion Symbolorum*, Barcelona, 1948, 179)

It is immediately apparent that, at least in his mode of expression, Chrysostom is far removed from the Council of Orange. Is the difference merely verbal, or is it doctrinal? In order to settle this question, it is necessary to give a summary of his whole teaching about grace.

I

That, in general, we need grace in order to live good lives, is a constant part of Chrysostom's teaching. He says that 'we always need a push from God if we are to be safely anchored' (*P. G.* 54, 672); all that we possess comes from God's grace (*P. G.* 61, 98). He insists on the necessity of prayer: 'Just as it is never inopportune to breathe, so it is never inopportune to pray. Rather, not to pray is inopportune. For just as we need breath, so we need his help' (*P. G.* 57, 307).

For what, precisely, is this help of God necessary? Chrysostom would answer: for τὸ κατορθοῦν, for ἀρετή. A *katorthoma*, as he uses the word, seems to be a morally good human action, pleasing to God, freely and meritoriously produced by someone who is already justified. Examples of *katorthomata* are: perseverance in faith; meekness; virginity.[1] *Areté* has a more vague and general meaning; in contrast to *katorthoma* it seems to mean a virtuous life rather than an act of virtue.[2]

Chrysostom constantly asserts that God's help is necessary for the performance of *katorthomata*. For instance he says: 'If we tried a thousand times, we should not be able to *katorthosai* anything unless we received also some push from above' (*P. G.* 54, 513); 'Our soul is quite insufficient for *katorthomata* unless we have received help' [from God] (*P. G.* 56, 182).[3]

Grace, then, is necessary for the performance of *katorthomata*. Chrysostom also teaches, by means of various metaphors, that without God's help we cannot reach heaven. When he is commenting on the Psalmist's words: 'Deduc me in tua justitia', he

---

1 In classical Greek κατορθοῦν meant 'to keep straight', 'to prosper', 'to succeed'; the noun κατόρθωμα is translated by Cicero as 'recte factum'. The word is not used in the NT. Chrysostom seems to use it in a Ciceronian sense: to do a right act. It is used in opposition to χάρισμα (*P. G.* 47, 558; 60, 398; 61, 98). In the *De prophetiarum obscuritate* (*P. G.* 56, 183) it is glossed as πράττειν τι τῶν τῷ θεῷ δοκούντων. Its meritorious and free aspect is stressed in the homily on *Habentes eundem spiritum fidei*, 4–5 (*P. G.* 51, 276). Examples of κατορθώματα given by Chrysostom are: not vacillating in faith (*P. G.* 60, 444); meekness (*P. G.* 54, 513); virginity (*P. G.* 47, 558). The texts in which Chrysostom uses the word usually refer to the morally virtuous acts *of the faithful* But faith is called a *katorthoma* in *P. G.* 51, 276; e contra, in 12 *in Cor.* 2 (*P. G.* 61, 98) Chrysostom denies that it is a *katorthoma*.

2 Chrysostom uses the word imprecisely. It is used of the penance of St Matthew (*P. G.* 54, 471); of man's part in virtue as opposed to God's (*P. G.* 61, 12 and elsewhere); of a virtuous life in general or a state of perfect virtue (*P. G.* 53, 228; 55, 426).

3 See also *P. G.* 53, 228; 57, 303; 63, 100.

explains that 'thy justice' means 'the justice which descends from thee, which leads to heaven'. Then he goes on:

> 'Lead' is very well said. The present life is a road, on which we need to be led by a heavenly hand. When we are going to enter a strange city, we need someone to show us the way. *A fortiori*, on our pilgrimage to heaven, we need guidance from above to direct us, to strengthen us, and lead us by the hand. (*P. G.* 55, 67)

Elsewhere he says that just as the Jews, on their return from the exile, needed God's help to rebuild Jerusalem, so we, who are entering on the road which leads to heaven, stand in even greater need of help (*P. G.* 55, 363). He expresses the same thought by a different metaphor when he says that we need the wings of the Spirit in order to be able to fly to heaven (*P. G.* 57, 29).

We have learnt so far that grace is necessary for acts of moral virtue, and for reaching heaven. Does Chrysostom also teach that grace is necessary for acts of all virtues, including faith, and for every step towards heaven, even the first? A full answer to this question must wait. Meanwhile it is sufficient to note that, though Chrysostom's common teaching is that grace is necessary for difficult acts, which it makes easier,[4] he also asserts that we need God's help in order to perform even easy actions. He says: 'It is not only in your labours and dangers that grace assists you; it cooperates with you even in those things which seem very easy [*in casu*: prayer]' (*P. G.* 60, 532).

The faithful, then, need divine help in order to perform virtuous actions. But Chrysostom is very insistent that these acts are to be attributed not only to God, but to man as well. Commenting on St Paul's words, 'vasa misericordiae, quae praeparavit [Deus] ad gloriam', he writes: 'When he says "which he had prepared for glory", he does not mean that the whole thing is God's. If this were so, nothing would prevent everybody being saved. Even if the greater part is God's nonetheless we too make our little contribu-

---

4 *P. G.* 50, 619 (martyrdom); 54, 655 (giving up one's son); 53, 228; 53, 385; 54, 471; 55, 432; 57, 254.

tion . . . Not everything is his even though heavenly grace is necessary' (*P. G.* 60, 561).[5] Chrysostom frequently says that our virtue is the fruit of some sort of cooperation between God and man. Thus: 'Virtue and vice are a matter of our own will, along with heavenly grace' (*P. G.* 54, 471); 'The zeal of man has no sufficiency by itself, unless he receives an influence from above; similarly, the heavenly influence is of no benefit to us, unless zeal be present also . . . Virtue is woven out of those two together' (*P. G.* 58, 742).[6]

Both God and man, then, contribute to the *katorthomata* of the faithful. It is time to examine more closely what it is that God contributes.

The words which Chrysostom uses to describe God's part are:

1. Χάρις or grace. This word does not have its technical post-Augustinian sense; it means every gift of God which is not owed to our merits, including, for instance, creation or the natural law.[7] In the texts which more nearly concern the questions which interest us, Chrysostom describes it as 'a gift of God' (*P. G.* 60, 400), which is 'spiritual' (*P. G.* 57, 29), which 'comes down from above' (*P. G.* 54, 471, 57, 303), which assists us and cooperates with us (*P. G.* 60, 416 and 532), which makes us God's debtors and crowns us (*P. G.* 57, 317; 60, 313). It is contrasted with our will or zeal (*P. G.* 54, 471; 57, 29; 57, 303; 60, 94; 60, 416).

2. The most general term is βοήθεια or help (*P. G.* 56, 182; 53, 228; 57, 303 and 307 and passim).

3. Metaphorically it is described in various ways: ἡ ανωθεν δεξια (*P. G.* 54, 471); ἡ ἄνωθεν χορηγία (*P. G.* 60, 532); ἡ ἄνωθεν χειραγωγία (*P. G.* 55, 67); πτερὸν τοῦ πνευματος (*P. G.* 56, 182; 57, 29).

---

5 There is an apparent contradiction in this text. The same dialectic is found in *P. G.* 47, 558; cf. 60, 416.

6 See also *P. G.* 55, 432; 55, 456; 57, 280; 62, 12.

7 See E. Boularand, S. J., 'La necessité de la grace pour arriver à la foi d'après S. Jean Chrysostome', *Gregorianum*, 19, 517ff.

Two expressions which Chrysostom frequently uses to describe God's influence on our actions are worth special attention because they throw light on the conception of grace which he had. They are ῥοπή and composite verbs containing συν-.

4. ῥοπή or ἡ ἄνωθεν ῥοπή (*P. G.* 54, 513; 55, 67; 59, 254; 60, 397; 63, 100 etc.). ῥοπή meant a weight which tilted a balance to one side or the other. If this metaphor is to be taken seriously, we must say that, for Chrysostom, God's influence is decisive but by no means prevenient. He seems to picture the matter thus: our good will, and the difficulty of doing good, are in different pans of a balance. They are more or less in equilibrium; but God's ῥοπή comes and tilts the balance over to the right side.

5. This conclusion is confirmed by other expressions which Chrysostom uses – especially verbs compounded of συν. Thrice he says that grace cooperates with us (συνεργάζεσθαι, *P. G.* 54, 471; 60, 416 and 532). Four times he describes the divine concursus as a συμμαχία or military alliance between God and man (*P. G.* 54, 513; 55, 432; 60, 532; 63, 100). His doctrine on this point is neatly summed up in the first chapter of the forty-second homily on Genesis (*P. G.* 53, 385). Chrysostom observes that the supporters of a pugilist in the Olympic games are allowed to cheer him, but not to help him. 'Our master is not like that. He fights with us (συναγωνίζεται) and stretches out his hand, and arms himself along with us; he does everything but hand over our adversary to us; he does all he can in his anxiety that we shall win the victory'. Here too, it seems that we are the first to begin the fight with the devil; when we have started, God enters the arena with us. His influence is decisive, but not prevenient. It is true that these texts are metaphorical, and perhaps should not be pressed; but it is almost always in metaphors that Chrysostom expresses his views, and in any case these conclusions will shortly be confirmed from another point of view.

We have seen what God contributes to man's virtue. Next we must examine the expressions which Chrysostom uses to describe man's share (τὰ παρ᾽ ἑαυτῶν, *P. G.* 53, 288; 53, 385; 57, 398, etc.).

1 προαίρεσις (decision or choice): *P. G.* 47, 408; 54, 471; 60, 416 & 556.
2 σπουδή (zeal, diligence, promptitude): *P. G.* 54, 513; 55, 432; 57, 280; 57, 398; 58, 472.
3 ἐπιμέλεια (diligence, care): *P. G.* 60, 107.
4 γνώμη (intention): *P. G.* 60, 559.
5 προθυμία (keenness): *P. G.* 57, 245; 58, 472 etc.
6 ἑλέσθαι, προελέσθαι, θέλειν, βούλεσθαι (choose, will): *P. G.* 60, 561 and passim.
7 εὐγνωμοσύνη (goodwill): *P.G.* 59, 354; 60, 561.

In general, therefore, Chrysostom seems to regard our part in virtue as being an internal act of the will. We will, choose; we display diligence or keenness; and God does the rest. Our part is a very small one; it is demanded only 'so that we may not be crowned without cause'. Chrysostom's view is prettily summarized in this text:

> This is why (God) wants you to do your small share of the work: so that the victory may be yours as well. Just as a king wants his son to stand in the line of battle, and brandish darts, and be conspicuous, so that he can be awarded a trophy, even though it is really himself who brings the war to victory: just so does God act in the war against the devil. He asks only one thing of you – to show enmity against him. If you grant him this, he will finish off the whole war. (*P.G.* 57, 254)

We have seen how Chrysostom conceives God's part and man's part in an act of virtue. We now come to the most important question. In this process, who has the initiative: man or God? Chrysostom answers: man. Man's part, even if it is a small part, is the first part. 'He who knows the secrets of our mind, when he sees that our mind is sound and that we are trying and striving to practise virtue, at once helps us by his approval and assistance' (*P. G.* 53, 385); 'If someone has zeal and keenness, then he will be given also those things which come from God. But if someone lacks these, and does not provide what he can provide, then he will not be given the things which come from God' (*P. G.* 57, 437); 'It is necessary that we should first choose the things which are good; and when we have chosen, then he contributes what is his' (*P. G.* 63, 100). There are similar passages scattered throughout Chrysostom's writings (e.g. *P. G.* 47, 408; 54, 513; 55, 456; 58, 472; 60, 651; 54, 432).

According to Chrysostom, then, virtue is woven together out of God's grace and man's resolve. God's grace has the greater part in this process, but it does not precede our election. Is this doctrine Pelagian, or semi-Pelagian? No, because what is in question is *katorthomata*, the acts of the man who is already justified. It is not heretical to say that man, once freely justified by God, can have the initiative in gaining an increase of grace. So that a Catholic could agree, without heresy, to all that we have seen hitherto in Chrysostom; though, after the Council of Orange, he would certainly want to express himself differently (he would wish to insist on the necessity of special grace for perseverance, for example). But equally, a semi-Pelagian could agree to all that we have seen. He could admit that a Christian, justified by his faith and by grace, needs God's help to perform acts of Christian virtue and to reach heaven.

The texts which we have hitherto discussed are, therefore, not *ad rem* in connection with the semi-Pelagian controversy. This negative conclusion is not a trivial one, since many writers have used some or other of these texts when giving an account of Chrysostom's doctrine about the *initium fidei*.

II

If we are to throw any light on the semi-Pelagian controversy, we must consider the texts in which Chrysostom is explicitly talking about faith. The question about the *initium fidei* cannot be solved *a priori* from a consideration of his general doctrine about grace.[8]

8 Boularand (l.c. pp. 518ff.), argues thus: For Chrysostom, grace gives us access, through the justice granted by baptism, to eternal life; hence it follows that the act of faith, the first step on the road to salvation, is an act of the supernatural order. Further, he holds that man is incapable of doing any good act without an 'impulse from on high'. Therefore he considers

There are some texts where Chrysostom seems to talk as if faith were an achievement of man alone. When he is commenting on the words of the Apostle, 'per ipsum habemus accessum ad fidem', he writes: 'I would like you to notice how he always puts these two things together – namely, what is from him, and what is from us. His contribution is multiform and various and great. He died for us, he reconciled us, he brought us up and gave us ineffable grace; while we contribute only faith' (*P. G.* 60, 468). And elsewhere, when he is praising Noe's virtues: 'Because he had first contributed what was his – namely, enthusiasm for virtue, strength of justice, and excellence of faith – therefore he received bountifully the things which are supplied by God, namely patience and fortitude . . . ' (*P. G.* 53, 228).

From these texts it looks as if Chrysostom considers faith as being the work of man alone, in no sense an effect of grace. But, as will soon become apparent, he does not mean that faith is 'ours' in an absolute sense, as if God had no share in it. He means that it is 'ours' in a relative sense, in comparison with patience, fortitude (which need greater grace) and with the merits of Christ. That he does in fact recognize faith as an effect of grace, becomes clear from the words which immediately follow, in the ninth homily on Romans, the first of the two texts just quoted. For immediately afterwards, he cites Paul's words, 'in fidem, in hanc gratiam in qua stamus', and goes on: '*Which* grace, I ask. That by which we are made free of the knowledge of God, by which we are freed from error, by which we know the truth, by which we receive everything through baptism' (*P. G.* 60, 468). So faith is not an achievement of man alone; God, too, plays a part in our acts of faith.

There are, as far as I have been able to discover, six texts where Chrysostom treats explicitly of the cooperation of God and man in the act of faith. Here they are:

---

that an impulse from on high is necessary for us to make an act of faith. This argument concludes only by substituting for the category *katorthoma* (which Chrys. uses) the category 'supernatural act' (which he does not). If it *did* conclude, it would make Chrysostom a semi-Pelagian, since he says that man has the initiative in the production of *katorthomata*.

1. The beginning of belief comes from our good will and from our obedience to the call; but after the foundation of faith has been laid then we need the help of the Spirit if faith is to remain in us unshakeable and unassailable. For neither God, nor the grace of the Spirit precedes our own resolution. Though he calls us, he waits for us to approach him spontaneously and of our own will. Then only, when we have approached, does he confer all his help on us. But how can we attract the help of the Spirit, and persuade him to stay with us? By good works and an excellent way of living (*Habentes eundem spiritum . . .* 4–5; *P. G.* 51, 276).

2. (Once again Chrysostom is explaining why Paul speaks of 'the spirit of faith' and not 'faith' *simpliciter*). He says this, to show that we need support if we are to reach the height of faith and learn to scorn the weakness of reasons . . . But perhaps someone will say – and it is indeed true – that he means the other sort of faith, by which miracles are performed. I too know that there is one sort of faith (about which the Apostles said: add faith to us) and another sort of faith, by means of which we are all 'the faithful', because we have knowledge of piety, even though we do not work miracles. Here also we need the help of the Spirit. For St Luke says about some woman: 'He opened her heart, that she might attend to those things which were said by Paul.' And Christ says: 'No one comes to me, unless the Father shall have drawn him.' If this therefore comes from God, how do they sin who do not believe, if the Spirit does not help them, nor the Father draw them, nor the Son lead them into the way? . . . How do they sin who are neither drawn, nor led, nor enlightened? Because they do not make themselves worthy to receive that enlightenment. See that this is what happened to Cornelius. He did not find this all by himself, but God called him, since he, first of all, had made himself worthy. And so Paul too, talking of faith, said: 'And this is not from you, it is a gift of God' – yet he did not leave you empty of good works. For although it belongs to him to draw and entice the soul, yet he seeks a soul which is prompt to obey, and then he contributes his help. For this reason too Paul says elsewhere: 'Those who are called

according to πρόθεσις.' For neither virtue, nor our salvation is subject to necessity (*Psal.* 115, 2; *P. G.* 55, 322).

3. 'Faith in me (Christ) is not a trivial affair, but needs an impulse from above'. Thus he gives a complete explanation of his words, showing that this faith needs a soul which is both generous and drawn by God. But perhaps someone will say: if everything which the Father gives comes to you, and no one can come to you unless it be given him from above, then those to whom the Father does not give are free from all blame or reproof. These are empty words and mere excuses. For we need also our own resolution. To learn and to believe belong to our resolution. In saying 'what the Father gives me' he means nothing else except that faith is not a chance affair, or the fruit of human reasoning, but needs both revelation from above, and a soul to receive it generously. (*John*, 3; *P. G.* 59, 254).

4. It is God who willed that we should be saved thus. For we did not achieve anything ourselves, but found salvation through the will of God. And we were called because it seemed good to him, not because we were worthy (1 *ad Cor*, 1; *P. G.* 81, 13).

5. (Commenting on 'Vocatis sanctis'). Even being saved by faith, he says, is not from you. For you did not approach first, but were called. So that even this little thing is not entirely yours. And even though you did approach though weighed down with thousands of evils, even so this is no thanks to you, but to God. It is for this reason that, writing to the Ephesians he said: 'You have been saved freely through faith, and this not from yourselves'; not even faith is entirely yours. For you did not take the initiative in believing, but obeyed when you were called (ibid.).

6 .Being virtuous, and believing, and approaching – this too comes from him who called. But it is ours too. But the fact that once we had approached, he thought us worthy to be brought straight from enmity to sonship: this comes from overflowing charity (*Eph*, 2; *P. G.* 62, 12).

A. All the texts agree, that in some stage at least of the process by which a man comes to faith, God's help is necessary.

B. All likewise agree that man too has his part to play in this process.

C. Faith, therefore, is the result of a cooperation between God and man. God's part in this cooperation is called βοήθεια (1, 2), χάρις (1), συμμαχία (1, 2), ῥοπή (3); i.e. it is described by the same words as the cooperation of God in acts of other virtues (cf. above). It is called also: ἀποκάλυψις (3), ἕλκειν (2, 3), ἐπαγαγεῖν (2), φωτίζειν (2) – that is to say, it is described by special metaphors. Especially it is called κλῆσις or vocation (1, 2, 4, 5, 6). Man's part is called εὐγνωμοσύνη (1, 3); βούλεσθαι (1), ἄξιον ἕαυτὸν παρασκευέσθαι (2), ψυχή εὐπειθής (2), ψυχή γενναῖα (3), προαίρεσις (1, 3) – just as his part in other virtues was. In particular, man's response to the divine vocation is called ὑπακοῦσαι (1, 4, 5) and προσελθεῖν (1, 5, 6). Therefore, in part, the cooperation between God and man in faith is described by the same words as all other cooperation. What is peculiar to this case, is the notion of vocation (κλῆσις) and of obedience (ὑπακοῦσαι,[9] προσελθεῖν). This notion, therefore, needs more accurate examination.

D. All the texts agree that for faith a divine vocation is necessary (except 3, which speaks instead of 'revelation').

E. If one considers all the texts together, κλῆσις seems to mean the first stage of divine intervention, in contrast to the other words which signify some second stage of divine operation, which follow man's activity (cf. especially 1, 5).

F. There seems, however, to be a contradiction between the first and the second of the texts we have quoted. In the first text, God's call precedes all act of disposition of man. In the second, man is called only after he has displayed a soul prompt to obey, after he has made himself worthy.

9 Note that ὑπακοῦσαι is described as belonging to man alone (4), while προσελθεῖν needs the aid of ὁ καλέσας (5, 6). The two words then cannot have quite the same meaning. Chrysostom is probably seeing the metaphor very concretely: God calls, man hears or obeys of himself, but in order to answer the call and approach the caller, he needs help.

How can we reconcile these texts? Only, it seems, by distinguishing two senses of the word κλῆσις.

(i) There is one vocation which is given to all men without exception. Chrysostom elsewhere says: 'If vocation were enough for salvation, why are not all saved? It is for this reason that (Paul) says that not vocation alone, but also the resolve of those who are called, works salvation. For vocation does not introduce necessity or any force. For all are called, but not all have obeyed' (*P. G.* 60, 541; *Hom.* 15 *in Rom*, 1).

(ii) There is also a particular vocation – a vocation to faith which can be compared with the special vocation of the Apostles. 'Paul always calls the faithful κλητοὶ ἅγιοι. For they have been called as far as faith; he, however, has received something else as well – namely the Apostolate' (*Rom*, 1; *P. G.* 60, 395).

Now the text which was cited first, from the homily on *Habentes eundem spiritum*, clearly refers to the general vocation, since it includes also unbelievers. The second text, however, from the commentary on Psalm 115, refers to the particular case of Cornelius, and therefore seems to be concerned with the particular vocation. There is therefore no contradiction between the two texts: the general vocation precedes man's act, the particular vocation follows it.

The general vocation corresponds to what we would call 'the salvific will of God'; the particular vocation corresponds to what we would call 'an efficacious vocation to faith'. In the semi-Pelagian controversy, what was in question was the particular and efficacious vocation; because even the semi-Pelagians would concede that the general salvific will of God precedes our merits. But the question they asked was: does the particular vocation of each man precede any act of his will?

To this question, the texts quoted from Chrysostom seem to give a negative reply. He explains the matter as follows. First, God calls all men to salvation, with a general vocation which can be rejected. Then man obeys this vocation, and makes himself worthy for a special vocation. Then only does God offer his help and give him a special vocation. So that, if we consider the situation of mankind in general, man does not have the initiative. But with regard to the particular case, he does. In a different terminology we might say that according to these texts there is gratuity of order, but not gratuity of election.

What now of the other texts, numbers 3–6 above? In these texts, the vocation precedes the obedience; and in 4 it is expressly said that we are called because God so willed, and not because we were worthy (So also the 22nd homily on St Matthew).

We must say that if these texts are concerned with the particular vocation, then they are fully orthodox on the lines of the Council of Orange. But if they are concerned with the general vocation, then they come to the same as the first two texts. I do not see how it can be settled for certain which of the two vocations Chrysostom had in mind when he wrote these two passages. However, there is one piece of evidence which suggests that he had in mind the general vocation, and therefore intended the less orthodox sense. That is, his teaching on predestination, to which we must now turn.

If you go through an index of Chrysostom's works, you will find very little *sub voce* 'Predestination'. This fact is itself not without significance. Indeed, Chrysostom does seem to have reduced predestination to mere prescience. When he asks, with Paul, why God loved Jacob and hated Esau, he says: 'Why did he love one, and hate the other? Why did one serve, and the other rule? Because one was evil, and the other good? But before they were born, one was honoured and the other condemned. Because they were still unborn, when God said that the elder should serve the younger. Why then did God say this? Because he does not wait, as a man does, to see from the course of events who is good and who is not; but already beforehand he knows who is evil and who is not' (*P. G.* 60, 555).

It is in a similar way that he explains the rejection of the Jews and the election of the Gentiles. He insists also that God's foreknowledge is not a cause of sin, nor of virtue. When he is explaining why an omniscient God *tests* man, he writes: 'Many who have a dull wit and are almost entirely lacking in intelligence say things like this: he chose this man, he loved this man, he hated that man, and that is why one turned out evil and the other turned out good. For this reason he persuades them by the facts themselves, testing people by their works, and correcting the error of this sort of person. Before anything comes to pass, he foretells that this man will be virtuous, so that people may realize his power of foreseeing; but he also tests men by their works, so that no-one may thoughtlessly say that a man is virtuous because of God's foreknowledge' (*P. G.* 55, 411). Predestination seems indeed to be reduced to mere prescience. God distributes graces equally. We could all do as well as St Paul, if only we had the will to do so: 'For if these men (the Apostles) turned out so wonderfully not because of their own resolve, but because of Christ's grace alone, what is to prevent us all becoming like them? . . . If grace did not require our operation first, it would have been poured abundantly into every one's heart: because God is not an acceptor of persons . . . Let us not deceive ourselves then, beloved, saying that not *anyone* can become like Paul. As far as grace and miracles are concerned, there will never be another Paul; but as far as perfection of life is concerned, anyone who willed it could be like him. If there never have been any such in fact, this is only because they did not want to be' (*P. G.* 47, 408).

In conclusion, it may be helpful to compare and contrast Chrysostom with the semi-Pelagians, or Massilienses. He has a great deal in common with them, both in background and in intention. Like them, he was a preacher and an ascetic, rather than a speculative theologian. Just as the Massilienses were afraid that Augustine's doctrine might cause negligence or despair in the faithful, so Chrysostom is anxious to explain the Pauline texts on predestination so that they will not leave room for carelessness.[10] Like them, he is above all preoccupied to see that the doctrine of grace is not taught in such a way as to diminish the freedom of the will.[11] Like them he is afraid that it may seem to follow from the

10 The Massilienses considered that Augustine's views 'et lapsis curam resurgendi adimere, et sanctis occassionem teporis afferre; eo quod in utraque parte superfluus labor sit, si neque rejectus ulla industria possit intrare, neque electus ulla negligentia possit excedere' (Prosper to Augustine, *P. L.* 33, 1003). For Chrysostom, see *P. G.* 47, 558; 62, 351f, and especially 58, 742.

11 The Massilienses said that Augustine 'introduced fate'. For Chrysostom, see *P. G.* 58, 472; 60, 599; 63, 100, and especially the nineteenth homily on Romans, c.1 (quod quaerit Israel, hoc non est consecutus).

doctrine of predestination that God is the author of sin and sinners are without fault.[12] These preoccupations, both in the case of Chrysostom and the Massilienses, are perfectly legitimate and orthodox.

However, both the Massilienses and Chrysostom establish a false parallelism between the election of those who are to be saved and the reprobation of those who are to be damned.[13] The Massilienses concluded from this parallelism that just as reprobation is not the cause of sin, so predestination is not the cause of salvation; and thus they reduce predestination to mere foreknowledge.[14] So, we have seen, does Chrysostom.

Both the Massilienses and Chrysostom (and also the Catholic faith, against Jansenius) insist that Christ died for all men without exception. From this the Massilienses and Chrysostom go on to draw the conclusion that the only thing which makes a difference between those who in fact will be saved and those who in fact will not, is human good or ill will.[15] The Massilienses concluded that the first step on the road to salvation comes from man alone;[16] and,

12 Cf. Chrysostom's rather embarrassed commentary on the passage about the potter's power over his clay in his sixteenth homily on Romans (*P. G.* 60, 559).

13 Massilienses: 'consequens putant, ut quia praevaricator ideo dicitur non obedisse, quia noluit, fidelis quoque non dubitetur ob hoc devotus fuisse, quia voluit' (*P. L.* 33, 1004.) Chrysostom: ὥσπερ οὖν ὁ Φαραὼ σκεῦος ὀργῆς γέγονεν ἀπὸ τῆς οἰκείας παρανομιας, οὕτω καὶ οὗτοι σκεύη ἐλέους ἀπὸ τῆς οἰκείας εὐγνωμοσύνης (*P. G.* 60, 561).

14 'Qui autem credituri sunt, quive in ea fide, quae deinceps per gratiam sit juvanda, mansuri sunt, praescisse ante mundi constitutionem Deum, et eos praedestinasse in regnum suum, quos gratis vocatos, dignos futuros electione, et de hac vita bono fine excessuros esse praeviderit' (*P. L.* 33, 1005).

15 Massilienses: 'Quantum ad Deum pertinet, omnibus paratam vitam aeternam; quantum autem ad arbitrii libertatem, ab his etiam apprehendi, qui Deo sponte crediderint, et auxilium gratiae merito credulitatis acceperint' (*P. L.* 33, 1005). Cf. Chrysostom: *Hom.* 16 *in Rom*, 5.

16 'Duo sunt quae humanam operantur salutem, Dei scilicet gratia et hominis obedientia; priorem volunt obedientiam esse quam gratiam, ut initium salutis ex eo qui salvatur, non ex eo credendum sit stare qui salvat' (*P. L.* 33, 1005).

as we have seen, there are texts of Chrysostom which seem to say the same.

It is also noteworthy that in Scriptural exegesis Chrysostom is often much closer to the interpretations given by the Massilienses than to those of Augustine. When St Paul speaks (Rom. 8:28) of those who 'secundum propositum vocati sunt', Chrysostom interprets this as referring to human resolve, not to God's decree. And the famous text, 'Miserebor cuius misereor', is glossed thus: 'It is not for you, Moses, to know who are worthy of my benevolence; that is my concern.'[17]

However, if there are similarities between Chrysostom and the Massilienses, there are also differences. The greatest difference is simply this: that they lived after the Pelagian controversy, while he lived before it. The whole position with regard to the problem of grace and freedom was not the same for them as for him.

1. Chrysostom does not draw a clear distinction between natural and supernatural actions. He did not therefore fall into the error which the Massilienses committed in thinking that a natural act could be the beginning of salvation.[18]

2. Chrysostom, as we have seen, said only hesitantly that the first step towards the salvation of the individual came from man alone. And he did not specify whether this first step was meritorious of grace, nor whether it was a positive or merely negative disposition. If, as is possible, he considered it merely as a negative disposition, then he is in line with post-Orange orthodoxy.[19] The Massilienses, on the other hand, thought that

---

17 See also, *P. G.* 58, 472; 60, 533, etc.

18 The Massilienses taught: '(hominem) ad hanc gratiam qua in Christo renascimur pervenire per naturalem scilicet facultatem petendo, quaerendo, pulsando: ut ideo accipiat, ideo inveniat, ideo introeat, quia bono naturae bene usus, ad istam salvantem gratiam initialis gratiae (creationis) ope meruerit pervenire' (*P.L.* 33, 1004).

19 I owe this point to Fr. Boularand (l.c., p. 539). However, though it is possible that Chrysostom meant his 'beginnings' to be mere negative dispositions or 'pretexts', it does not seem very likely. His list of the things which man contributes to the act of faith ('making himself worthy', 'the

man's first step strictly merited God's help.[20]

3. Chrysostom never clearly distinguished between vocation and election (as we have seen, he used the same word to describe both). The Massilienses, on the other hand, distinguished very clearly, and considered vocation to be gratuitous, while election they regarded as a reward for merit.[21]

In conclusion, then, it seems that we must say this: It would be wrong to call Chrysostom a semi-Pelagian, because, for lack of the necessary distinctions, he never posed himself the problem about the *initium fidei* in the way in which they did. However, this too seems to be true: that there is nothing in his works with which the Massilienses would have disagreed, while there is a great deal which no Catholic, after the Council of Orange, would dare to say.

---

beginning of belief', 'resolutions', 'good works', 'excellent behaviour', etc.) seems to include rather more than negative dispositions. Indeed it seems dangerously near to contradicting the Council of Orange which says that we need grace in order to 'credere, desiderare, conari, laborare, vigilare, studere, petere, quarere, pulsare, ut oportet'. It is true, as Boularand says, that man's part is sometimes described by the word ἀφορμαι, which he translates (p. 535) as 'pretextes'. But when the very same word is applied to *God's part* in our salvation, he translates it 'moyens'! (p. 536).

20 Cf. footnote 18; also *P. L.* 33, 1007.

21 They taught '(Deum) eos praedestinasse in regnum suum quos gratis vocatos, dignos futuros electione, et de hac vita bono fine excessuros esse praeviderit' (*P. L.* 33, 1003).

8

Aquinas on Divine Foreknowledge and Human Freedom

In this paper I intend to discuss whether belief in God's foreknowledge of the future is compatible with belief in the freedom of human actions. Before stating the problem in further detail, I must make clear which problems I do *not* intend to consider. I shall not discuss whether there is a God, nor whether it is the case that some human actions are free. I shall not try to show that an action which is causally determined is not free, nor that God knows the future free actions of men. It might be thought, indeed, that this last at least needs no proving: surely, if there is a God at all, He knows all that is to come; a God who did not know the future would not be a real God. But this is not so. It is indeed the case that any God worthy of the name knows everything that there is to be known; but it does not follow from this alone that He knows the future free actions of men. For many philosophers have maintained, and some do maintain, that statements about as yet undecided free actions, such as the statement 'The United States will declare war on China', are as yet neither true nor false. Since only what is true can be known, then if it is not yet true either that the US will declare war on China nor that the US will not declare war on China, then not even God can know whether the US will do so or not. Again, as a matter of history there have been philosophers who have believed that God was omniscient without thereby believing that God knew the future free actions of men. Indeed, as we shall see, even a philosopher so orthodox as St Thomas Aquinas denied, in one important sense, that God knows the future when the future is not already determined by causal necessity. Even to theists, therefore, it needs to be proved that God knows what is going to take place through the free action of his creature. As I have said, I do not intend to argue for this. I intend merely to investigate whether there is or is not compatibility between two statements, namely, 'God knows beforehand everything that men will do' and 'Some actions of men are free'. Even in this restricted area I intend to examine only two arguments which have been brought up to show that the statements are incompatible. The question of incompatibility retains its interest for philosophers even if both statements are in fact false.

It is necessary, as a final preamble, to insist that the problem to be discussed concerns only foreknowledge and not foreordaining. Just as people have believed that God knows beforehand all that happens in the world, so also they have believed that He ordains beforehand all that happens in the world. Just as no human action escapes God's prescience, so no human action escapes His providence. Accordingly, just as there is a problem how God's foreknowledge may be reconciled with human freedom, so also there is a problem how human freedom may be reconciled with God's providence. In particular, since according to traditional Christian belief, no-one is saved who is not predestined by God to be saved, those who accept that belief have a special problem in reconciling it with the belief that those who are damned are damned through their own fault. These further problems are interesting, complicated and difficult; but they will not be our concern in this paper.

The problem may be stated as follows. God's foreknowledge appears to be incompatible with human freedom. It does not seem to be possible both that God should know what I shall do in the future, and that I shall do freely whatever it is that I shall do. For in order for me to be able to do an action freely, it is necessary that it should be within my power not to do that action. But if God knows what my action is going to be before I do it, then it does not seem to be within my power not to do it. For it cannot be the case both that God knows that I shall do such and such an action, and that I shall not in fact do it. For what God knows must be true: and indeed what anybody knows must be true, since it is impossible to know what is false. But if what God knows is true, and God knows that I will do such and such an action, then it must be true that I will do it. And if it is true that I will do it, then it seems that nothing I can do can prevent it coming true that I am doing it. And if nothing I can do can prevent it coming true that I am doing it, then I cannot prevent myself doing it. And if I cannot prevent myself doing a certain action, then that action cannot be free. Therefore, either God cannot know what I shall do tomorrow, or else whatever I shall do tomorrow will not be done freely.

For example: if God knows now that I will tell a lie this time tomorrow, then it seems that I cannot be free not to tell a lie this time tomorrow. For it cannot be the case both that God knows that I will tell a lie tomorrow, and that I will not in fact tell a lie tomorrow. For what God knows must be true: so that if God knows that I will tell a lie tomorow, it must be true that I will tell a lie tomorrow. But if it must be true that I will tell a lie tomorrow, then I cannot be free not to tell a lie tomorrow. But if I am not free not to tell a lie tomorrow, then when tomorrow I tell a lie, I shall not do so freely. A similar argument appears to hold, no matter what human action we consider instead of telling lies. Therefore it seems that if God foresees all human actions, no human action can be free.

This difficulty is a very old one. It is stated, for instance, in St Thomas Aquinas' *Summa Theologiae*, Ia 14, 3, 3. Aquinas' statement of the difficulty is as follows: 'Whatever is known by God must be; for whatever is known by us must be, and God's knowledge is more certain than ours. But nothing which is future and contingent *must* be. Therefore, nothing which is future and contingent is known by God.' This difficulty is recognizably the same as the one which I have just stated more verbosely. The only difference of importance is that while I spoke of future free actions, St Thomas speaks of future contingent events. St Thomas uses the word 'contingent' as equivalent to 'not causally determined'. Assuming that no causally determined action is a free action, a free human action would be a contingent event within the meaning of St Thomas' phrase. Indeed St Thomas expressly states (ibid., *Sed contra*) that free human actions are contingent events. He thought also that there were other contingent events besides free human actions: the budding of a tree, for instance. Whether he was correct in thinking this is an interesting question, but not to our purpose.

To the difficulty which he has set, St Thomas provides a long answer. Part of his answer runs as follows. 'The proposition "whatever is known by God must be" can be analysed in two ways. It may be taken as a proposition *de dicto* or as a proposition *de re*; in other words, it may be taken either *in sensu composito* or *in sensu diviso*. As a *de re* proposition, it means:

Of everything which is known by God, it is true that that thing must be.

So understood the proposition is false. As a proposition *de dicto* it means:

The proposition "whatever God knows is the case" is necessarily true.

So understood, the proposition is true.'

There is much more in St Thomas' answer than this paragraph, but this argument, as it stands, seems to me an adequate answer to the difficulty. In order to understand it one must know something about the medieval distinction between propositions *de dicto* and propositions *de re*. Consider the following proposition.

1. If there is a University at Oxford, then necessarily there is a University at Oxford.

Someone who asserts that proposition may be taken to assert

2. 'If there is a University at Oxford, then there is a University at Oxford' is a necessary truth.

Or he may be taken to assert

3. If there is a University at Oxford, then 'there is a University at Oxford' is a necessary truth.

The medievals would have called proposition 1, if interpreted in the sense of proposition 2, a proposition *de dicto*; if interpreted in the sense of proposition *de re*. The difference between the two interpretations is obviously of crucial importance. For 2, which merely states that a certain conditional – whose consequent is a repetition of its antecedent – is necessarily true, it itself true. But 3 is false, since its antecedent is true (there is a University at Oxford), and its consequent is false (it is not a necessary truth that there is a University at Oxford, since there has not always been a University at Oxford).

It is not difficult to see how to apply this to the problem in hand. The proposition 'Whatever is known by God is necessarily true' if taken *de dicto* means

4. 'Whatever is known by God is true' is a necessary truth.

Interpreted *de re*, however, it means.

5. Whatever is known by God is a necessary truth.

Proposition 4 is true, but it has no tendency to show that acts foreseen by God are not free. For, it is equally a necessary truth that if I will tell a lie this time tomorrow, then I will tell a lie this time tomorrow: but this necessary truth has no tendency to show that my telling of a lie tomorrow will not be free. On the other hand, 5 if true would rule out the possibility of free action. If it is a necessary truth that I will tell a lie tomorrow, then I have no choice in the matter. But this need not trouble us; for proposition 5 is simply false. If God knows everything, then God knows that I am now writing this paper; but 'I am writing this paper' is not a necessary truth, since it was in fact false ten days ago. We might bring out the difference between the two interpretations of 'whatever is known by God is necessarily true' by punctuation, as follows.

4a. Whatever is known by God is, necessarily, true.
5a. Whatever is known by God is necessarily-true.

It seems to me, therefore, that St Thomas' answer to this particular difficulty is entirely satisfactory. But he puts to himself a further, and more persuasive, difficulty; and his answer to this second difficulty does not appear satisfactory at all.

The further difficulty runs as follows. In any true conditional proposition whose antecedent is necessarily true, the consequent is also necessarily true. That is to say, whatever is implied by a necessary proposition is itself a necessary proposition. The following is clearly a true conditional proposition: 'If it has come to God's knowledge that such and such a thing will happen, then such and such a thing will happen.' The antecedent of the conditional, if it is true at all, appears to be necessarily true: for it is in the past tense, and what is past cannot be changed. What has been the case cannot now not have been the case. Therefore, the consequent is also necessarily true. Therefore, whatever is known by God is a necessary truth.

This is a powerful argument: it appears, at least at first sight, impossible to deny any of its premises. St Thomas himself treated it with great respect: before putting forward his own solution he considered and rejected three attempts to deny one or other premise. In the end, he could find no alternative to accepting the argument, while trying to show that the conclusion is not, as it appears to be, incompatible with the occurrence of contingent events.

His solution runs as follows. God, he says, is outside time: God's life is measured not by time, but by eternity. Eternity, which has no parts, overlaps the whole of time; consequently, the things which happen at different times are all present together to God. An event is known *as future* only when there is a relation of future to past between the knowledge of the knower and the happening of the event. But there is no such relation between God's knowledge and any contingent event: the relation between God's knowledge and any event in time is always one of simultaneity. Consequently, a contingent event, as it comes to God's knowledge, is not future but present; and as present it is necessary; for what is the case, is the case, and is beyond anyone's power to alter. Hence, we can admit that what is known to God is a necessary truth; for as known by God it is no longer future but present. But this necessity does not destroy contingency: for the fact that an event is necessary when it happens does not mean that it was predetermined by its causes.

St Thomas adds plausibility to his solution with a famous illustration.

> To us, because we know future contingent events as future, there can be no certainty about them; but only to God, whose knowing is in eternity, above time. A man who is walking along a road cannot see those who are coming after him; but a man who looks down from a hill upon the whole length of the road can see at the same time all those who are travelling along it. So it is with God . . . Future events which are in themselves contingent cannot be known to us. What is known to God is necessary in the way in which it lies open to God's knowledge (namely, in its presentness); it is not necessary in regard to its own causes.[1]

This explanation of St Thomas has become the classic solution of the problem raised by God's foreknowledge. It is still sometimes presented in popular expositions of Christian theology, for instance in *Theology and Sanity* by F. J. Sheed. 'If God knew last Tuesday what you were going to do next Tuesday, what becomes of your free will? . . . God did *not* know *last* Tuesday. Tuesday is a period of time and part of the duration in which I act. But God acts in eternity which has no Tuesdays. God acts in the spacelessness of his immensity and the timelessness of his eternity: we receive the effects of his acts in space and time' (p. 117).

Despite the authority of St Thomas, the solution seems fundamentally misconceived. In the first place, it forces one to deny that it is true, in any strict sense, that God knows future free actions. St Thomas insists repeatedly that no-one, not even God, can know contingent events *qua* future: he says of such events that we should rather say 'if God knows something, then it *is*' than 'if God knows something, then it *will be*' (*De Veritate* 2, 12 ad 7). Strictly speaking, then, God has no *fore*knowledge of contingent events: as He knows

---

1 *Summa Theologiae*, 14, 13 ad 3 (words in brackets from the body of the article). The preceding paragraph is a mosaic of translations from *De Veritate* 2, 12.

them, they are not still future but already present. A defender of St Thomas might reply that this does not matter: when we say that God knows future events we mean merely that (a) God knows all events, and (b) some events are future *to us*. Of any event which is future to us it will be true to say that God knows it, though he will not know it *qua* future. Thus, let us suppose that at some future date a person will land on Mars. The event which is the landing on Mars is, so far as we are concerned, in the future; but to God it is already present. Thus, although we cannot say that God knows that a person *will* land on Mars (for this would be to make God know it *qua* future) we can say that God knows, timelessly, the event which is the landing on Mars. And this event is future to us, that is to say, it comes later in the time series than, for example, your reading this.

But this reply does not meet the objection. If 'to know the future' means know more than 'to know a fact which comes later in the time series than some other fact' then we, no less than God, can know the future. For we know about the Wars of the Roses which *were* future when Cleopatra was a girl. If we were to take St Thomas' suggestion seriously, we should have to say that God knows that a person *is landing* on Mars; but we cannot say this, since the statement that a person is landing on Mars, being false, cannot be known, even by God, to be true.

St Thomas' solution then, is not so much a defence as a denial of God's foreknowledge. But it forces us to deny not only God's foreknowledge, but also God's omniscience. For the statement that God's foreknowledge is outside time must mean, if anything, that no temporal qualifications can be attached to God's knowledge. Where God is the subject, verbs of knowing cannot have adverbs of time affixed to them. We cannot, therefore, say that God knows now that Brutus killed Caesar; nor that God will know tomorrow what time I went to bed tonight. But as A. N. Prior has remarked, it seems an extraordinary way of affirming God's omniscience if a person, when asked what God knows *now*, must say 'Nothing', and when asked what he knew yesterday, must again say 'Nothing', and must yet again say 'Nothing' when asked what God will know *tomorrow*.

An argument *ad hominem* against St Thomas' position may be

drawn from the notion of prophecy. St Thomas believed that God could foretell, and had foretold, future contingent events. He believed, for example, that God, as the principal author of the Epistle to the Romans, had foretold the conversion of the Jewish people to Christianity. On the view that God's knowledge is timeless, such prediction becomes inexplicable. For, if God's knowledge is timeless, then we cannot attach to statements about God's knowledge such adverbial clauses as 'at the time when the Epistle to the Romans was written'. We cannot, for example, say 'At the time when the Epistle to the Romans was written God already knew that the Jews would finally be converted'. But if God did not then know it, how could he then foretell it? To put it bluntly: if God did not then *know* that the Jews would be converted, he had no right then to *say* that they would.

Indeed, the whole concept of a timeless eternity, the whole of which is simultaneous with every part of time, seems to be radically incoherent. For simultaneity as ordinarily understood is a transitive relation. If *A* happens at the same time as *B*, and *B* happens at the same time as *C*, then *A* happens at the same time as *C*. If the BBC programme and the ITV programme both start when Big Ben strikes ten, then they both start at the same time. But, on St Thomas' view, my typing of this paper is simultaneous with the whole of eternity. Again, on his view, the great fire of Rome is simultaneous with the whole of eternity. Therefore, while I type these very words, Nero fiddles heartlessly on.

If St Thomas' solution to the difficulty is unacceptable, is it possible to give a different one? The objection ran thus. What is implied by a necessary proposition is itself necessarily true. But from 'it has come to God's knowledge that such and such will be the case' it follows that 'such and such will be the case'. But 'it has come to God's knowledge that such and such will be the case' is necessarily true; therefore 'such and such will be the case' is necessarily true. Therefore, if God knows the future, the future is not contingent.[2]

The premises of the argument appear difficult to deny; yet if its

2 Using '*Lp*' for 'Necessarily *p*', '*Gp*' for 'It has come to God's knowledge that *p*', and '*Cpq*' for 'If *p*, then *q*' we could symbolize the argument thus: *LCLCGppLCLGpLp*; *LCGpp*; *LGp*; ergo, *Lp*.

conclusion is true there is no freedom or else no foreknowledge. For if it must be the case that I will murder my grandfather, then I am not free not to murder my grandfather; and conversely, if I am free not to murder my grandfather, then God cannot know that I will murder him even if in fact I will do so.

Let us examine each premise in turn. It appears incontroverible that what follows from a necessary proposition is itself necessary.[3] Moreover, it cannot be denied that 'it is the case that p' follows from 'It has come to God's knowledge that p': this is true *ex vi termini* 'know'. So, for any substitution for 'p', if 'It has come to God's knowledge that p' is necessarily true, then 'it is the case that p' is also necessarily true.

But is it true, for all substitutions for 'p', that it must be the case that it has come to God's knowledge that p? St Thomas accepted it without question. 'It has come to God's knowledge that p' is a proposition in the past tense, and for St Thomas as for Aristotle all propositions in the past tense are necessary. Now let us first notice that even if this doctrine were true, there has occurred a significant change in the sense of 'necessary'. Hitherto, 'necessarily' has been used in such a way that in every case it could have been replaced by 'it is a logical truth that . . .' But if an Aristotelian claims that 'Cesare Borgia was a bad man' is now necessarily true, he must be using 'necessarily' in a different sense. For he cannot claim that it is a logical truth that Cesare Borgia was a bad man. Again, let us notice, that the necessity of past propositions, if they are necessary, is not something that is *eo ipso* incompatible with freedom. If it is now necessary that Cesare Borgia was a bad man, it does not follow from this alone that it was, when he was born, necessary that the *would* be a bad man. For, according to Aristotle, necessity applies only to true past and present propositions, not to future propositions of contingent fact. But, when Cesare Borgia was born, the proposition 'Cesare Borgia will be a bad man' was a future-tensed proposition of contingent fact – as indeed it still is.

It is clear, then, that if present- and past-tensed propositions are, as Aristotle thought, necessary in a way in which future-tensed propositions are not, they are not necessary in the way in which

3 *LCLCpqLCLpLq* is a law in every standard modal system.

logical truths are necessary; and they are not necessary in a way which excludes the freedom of the ation they report, if they report an action at all.

But is there any sense at all in which past- and present-tensed propositions have a necessity which is not shared by future-tensed propositions? The very least which seems to be demanded of a proposition if it is to be called 'necessary' is that it is always has been, and always will be, true. In this sense of 'necessary' the proposition 'there is a God' is necessarily true if it is true at all; but of course the proposition 'there is a God' is not a logical truth, as critics of the ontological argument, from Gaunilo to Russell, have frequently pointed out. Now the proposition 'Queen Anne is dead', which is a true present-tensed proposition if ever there was one, is not a necessary truth in this sense at all, since before 1714 it was not true. The past-tensed proposition 'Queen Anne has died' will indeed never cease to be true; but it *was* not true in King Alfred's day. So, even if 'necessary' is given the weak interpretation of 'true at all times', there seems no reason to believe the Aristotelian doctrine that past- and present-tensed propositions *in materia contingenti* are necessary.

Yet is it not true that what has happened cannot now not have happened, and that which is happening cannot now not be happening? We have a very strong inclination to think that there is some way in which we can change the future, in which we cannot change the past. But this inclination appears to be a delusion. There appears to be no sense in which we can change the future in which we cannot change the past. As A. N. Prior has pointed out, whatever changes of plan we may make, the future is whatever takes place after all the changes are made; what we alter is *not* the future, but our plans; the real future can no more be altered than the past. The sort of case which we have in mind when we are tempted to say that we can change the future is this: suppose that I have no intention of typing 'elephant' backwards; then I decide I will do so; and finally I do so. Does not my decision change the future, since without my decision the word would never have been typed backwards? No, for even when I had no intention of doing so, e.g. ten years ago, it *was* true that I would, ten years later, type 'elephant' backwards; and so my decision altered nothing except my own intentions. There is, indeed, a sense in which we can change the future: we can change the truth-value of a future-tensed proposition. Suppose that it is true that I will commit suicide: then the proposition 'A. K. will commit suicide' now has the truth-value 'true'. I can change this truth-value by committing suicide; for once I have committed suicide the proposition 'A. K. will commit suicide' ceases to be true and the quite different proposition 'A. K. has committed suicide' becomes true instead. But if 'to change the future' means merely 'to change the truth-value of a future-tensed proposition' then in a corresponding sense I can change the past no less than the future. Nothing is easier. Tnahpele. The past-tensed proposition 'A. K. has typed "elephant" backwards' which *was* false, is now true; and so I have changed the past.

It seems, then, that there is no sense in which we can change the future in which we cannot change the past. Still, it does seem true that we can bring about the future, but cannot bring about the past; our present activity may have a causal effect on the future but cannot have a causal effect on the past. Consequently deliberation about the future is sensible, deliberation about the past absurd; so if God's knowledge of what I will do tomorrow is already a thing of the past, deliberation about what I will do tomorrow appears already pointless, and once again there appears to be an incompatibility between foreknowledge and freedom.

However, in certain cases, it does seem that present actions can affect the past. By begetting a son, I make my grandfather, long dead, into a great-grandfather; by becoming Poet Laureate I make my late grandmother's belief that I would one day be Poet Laureate into a true belief. In such cases, of course, what we are doing is establishing new relations between past things and events and present or future things or events. But the truth of a belief, and the question of whether a certain belief does or does not constitute knowledge, involve relationships between those beliefs and the events they concern. So it is possible that it is precisely by telling a lie today that I bring it about that God knew yesterday that I would tell a lie today. Of course, I do not bring it about by today's lie that God yesterday *believed* that I would lie; but it is my current lie which makes his belief then true.

Even so, it might be retorted, this does not make it possible for God to have *known* yesterday without curtailment of my freedom; because knowledge is not true belief, but justified true belief; and the justification of a past belief would have to be past grounds for the belif; and nothing in the past could be adequate grounds for a belief about my current action unless it necessitated that action. To this the reply is open that even in non-theological contexts there seem to be cases where true belief, without grounds, constitutes knowledge. One such case is our knowledge of our own actions. Commonly, we know what we are doing with our hands, and we do not know this on the basis of any evidence or grounds. Of course, we can be mistaken: I may think I am typing 'piece' and in fact be typing 'peice'. But when I am not mistaken, my belief about what I am doing constitutes knowledge. It does not seem unreasonable to suggest that in this respect a Creator's knowledge of his creature's actions might resemble a human agent's knowledge of his own actions.

There seems, then, no reason to maintain that 'It has come to God's knowledge that p' is a necessary truth, in any of the senses we have suggested, merely because it is past-tensed. Might it not be argued, however, that it is a necessary truth for a different reason: namely, that it is a truth about God's knowledge, which is the knowledge of a necessarily omniscient necessary being? If God is omniscient, it might be argued, then whatever we substitute for 'p', 'it has come to God's knowledge that p' will be true. But 'if it has come to God's knowledge that p' is true no matter what we substitute for 'p', then it must be something like a logical truth, and so a necessary truth in the sense in which necessity is incompatible with freedom.

It does not take a moment to detect the fallacy in this argument. God's omniscience does not at all imply that whatever we substitute for 'p' in 'God knows that p' is true. For instance, if we substitute '$2 + 2 = 3$' we get not a necessary truth but the falsehood 'God knows that $2 + 2 = 3$'. It is indeed a logical truth that if p is true, then p is known by any omniscient being; but this is insufficient to provide the premise needed by St Thomas' objector.[4]

4 We have not LGp but $LCpGp$.

A sentence such as 'God knows that I am sitting down' expresses not a necessary, but a contingent truth: it may be true now, but it was not true last night and it will cease to be true as soon as I stand up. In fact, God's knowledge will only be necessary where what He knows is necessary: '2 + 2 = 4' is a necessary truth, so 'God knows that 2 + 2 = 4' is a necessary truth.[5] But, by definition, a contingent proposition – such as a proposition reporting or predicting a free action – is never a necessary truth. Hence, the argument that we have been considering has no tendency to show that human freedom and divine foreknowledge are incompatible.

There are other arguments to prove this incompatibility: Aquinas alone gives thirteen of which we have considered only two. None, however, are as initially plausible, or as complicated to unravel, as the two we have considered.

5 We have not *LCpLGp*, but *LCLpLGp*.

9

Realism and Determinism
in the Early Wyclif

Wyclif has long had a reputation as an extreme determinist. One of the doctrines for which he was condemned by the Council of Constance was the proposition that everything happens by absolute necessity.[1] Throughout the fifteenth and early sixteenth centuries his career was seen as a warning by orthodox theologians, and one of the reasons why he was a bogey-man was because he was held to be an extreme necessitarian. At Louvain theologians, in order to avoid the pitfalls of Wycliffism, went so far as to toy with three-valued logic.[2]

Historians of ideas sometimes tell us that Wyclif was an extreme determinist because he was a realist. His realism, we are told, left no room for the contingency and unpredictability of human action or other undetermined behaviour.

In this paper I want to cast doubt on both these familiar ideas. I shall question whether Wyclif really was a determinist in any way which rules out the degree of freedom allotted to humans by other theologians. And I shall argue that even if it is true that Wyclif, early or late in his career, was a determinist, it is certainly not true that his determinism was derived from his realism.

I shall proceed by examining in some detail the fourteenth

---

1 'Omnia de necessitate absoluta eveniunt' Denzinger, *Enchiridion Symbolorum*, 371.

2 L. Baudry, *La Querelle des Futurs Contingents* (Paris, 1950).

chapter of Wyclif's *De Universalibus*, one of his fullest and most enlightening discussions of the relevant topics.[3] A study of this chapter shows that he was not, at the time of writing it, a determinist in any anti-libertarian sense. This does not show that he did not become one at some later period of his life; but it does show that if he did so it was because he must have ceased to regard as important a number of distinctions which he makes at this period with great care and skill. Moreover, it shows that if ever he became a determinist it was not because of his realism. For the *De Universalibus* is the fullest statement of his realism, and is quite free of any vicious determinism.

The realism of the *De Universalibus* is most concisely summed up in the thesis that there are four kinds of being which creatures may have. The first is as an Idea in the mind of God. This is their most exalted being: so considered, a creature is an item of divine life. As we read in the Prologue of the Fourth Gospel 'What was made, in Him was life'. Secondly, Wyclif says, creatures have being in their causes: this is called essential being. Causes may be general or particular. The general causes are the kinds or species which God made when the world began; once a species is created, every individual has one type of being in the relevant species as its universal cause. According to Christian teaching, all men belong not only to the same species, but to the same stock, being descended from a single Adam. In Adam, then, they have being as in their particular cause. Thus all humans who have ever lived or will ever live have essential being in humankind and in their first progenitor.[4]

There is a third kind of being: this is what we would nowadays call 'existence'.

> Thirdly, creatures have a being which is the existence of the individual, which begins to be and ceases to be at its own time. This is the only being which modern doctors accept. But

3 *Tractatus de Universalibus*, text edited by Ivan J. Mueller, translated by Anthony Kenny (Oxford, 1985). References to this work are given by 'U' followed by the chapter and line number (which is the same in both Latin and English texts).
4 U, VII, 35–54.

even recent writers grant, with respect to the second being, that even when there are no roses in existence a rose is a flower . . . For it is one thing to be, and another to exist.[5]

The fourth mode of being is accidental being: the possession by a substance of a non-essential property such as a transitory colour. Accidental being comes and goes during the lifetime of its subject.

Thus, then, every creature can have four kinds of being: ideal being in the mind of God; essential being in causes; existential being or existence in itself; and accidental being in its ephemeral qualities.

Now the kind of being which is peculiar to Wyclif, and which marks him out as a realist, is the second kind of being: essential being in universal causes. But the kind of being which makes difficulties for freedom and contingence is the first kind of being: ideal being in the mind of God. The problem of necessity and liberty is not set by Wyclif's own system, but by a framework of ideas common to all medieval theologians. We can see this if we turn for a moment to the theologian whom Wyclif revered more than any other medieval: Grosseteste.[6]

In his *De Libero Arbitrio* Grosseteste discusses a problem which we can present, in modern idiom, as follows. Let '*p*' abbreviate some future contingent proposition such as 'Antichrist will come'. Then consider the following argument: 'If God knows that *p*. then *p*. God knows that *p*. Therefore, *p*.' Each of the premises of this argument, it seems, is necessarily true. The conclusion necessarily follows from the premises. Therefore the conclusion is necessary, and not contingent as we had assumed.[7]

---

5 Tertio habet creatura esse existere individuum, secundum quod esse incipit et corrumpitur pro suo tempore. Et solum illud esse acceptant moderni doctores. Vero etiam recentes concedunr iuxta secundum esse quod nulla rosa existente, rosa est flos . . . Aliud enim est esse et aliud existere. U, VII, 55–64.

6 Grosseteste's *De Libero Arbitrio* has been edited by L. Baur, *Die philosophischen Werke des Robert Grosseteste* Beiträge zur Geschichte der Philosophie des Mittelalters 9 (1912) 150–241.

7 BGPM, 9, p. 152.

Surely we cannot deny the necessity of the first premise. But is the second necessary? Some have said that it is not even true, alleging that God knows only universals and not particular truths: but that is impious.[8] Others have argued that it is false on the grounds that knowledge is of what there is, but future contingents are not there to be known. But that is unacceptable, because it would make God's knowledge something which alters from time to time.

Shall we say, then, that the second premise is true but contingent? If it is contingent that God knows that p, then it seems that he knows that p, but *can* not know that p. But if so, then it seems that he can pass from knowing that p to not knowing that p. But that would make his knowledge, once again, something that is subject to alteration.[9]

There is, indeed, a sense in which God's knowledge is subject to alteration; but it is a harmless one which does not conflict with divine immutability. Grosseteste offers the following sophism to illustrate his point. 'God knows that I will sit. But once I have sat he will no longer know that I will sit, but that I have sat. So he now knows something which later he will not know.' This, Grosseteste says, does not prove the alterability of God's knowledge of 'the essences of things not taken in relation to the vicissitudes of tenses'.[10]

But if we leave aside the complications of tense, we must say that whatever God now knows he cannot later not know. This is so no matter whether the object of his knowledge is in existence or not. Neither 'Antichrist will come' nor 'God knows that Antichrist will come' can change from being true to being false. For suppose they did become false. Then 'Antichrist will come' would be false; and if false, it must always have been false. Hence it cannot change from

8 BGPM, 9, pp. 152–8.

9 BGPM, 9, pp. 158–9.

10 Nec fiat vis de huiusmodi sophismatibus: Deus scit me sessurum et non sciet me sessurum, postquam sedi, sed sedisse. Ergo scit aliquid quod non sciet. Hoc autem non sequitur, quia in ipsum non cadit temporum vicissitudo, sed abstractis omnibus conditionalibus temporalibus scit. Eius enim scientia cadit super ipsas essentias rerum non relatas ad temporum mutationes. BGPM, pp. 159–60.

being true to being false (in any way other than by coming true).[11]

So it seems that we cannot deny the necessity of either the first or the second premise. Must we say then either that everything is necessary or that what is necessarily entailed by necessary truths need not itself be necessary?[12]

The solution, for Grosseteste, lies in distinguishing between two kinds of necessity. There is a stronger kind of necessity and a weaker kind. In the stronger sense, it is necessary that p if it is not possible that it should ever, at any time, have been the case that not-p. In the weaker sense, p is necessary if it is not possible that it should become the case that not p. The stronger kind of necessity involves sempiternal truth; the weaker kind involves only immutable truth.[13]

With this distinction, Grosseteste attempts to disarm the argument against contingency. The first premise is no doubt strongly necessary, but the second premise is only weakly necessary: God cannot now change to not knowing that p, but it might have been the case from all eternity that he did not know that p. We can agree that what follows from what is necessary is itself necessary in the same sense as its premises are; but since one of the premises is only weakly necessary, the conclusion is only weakly necessary, and the lack of strong necessity suffices, Grosseteste maintains, for freedom.[14]

Wyclif, like Grosseteste, attempts to resolve the paradoxes of freedom and foreknowledge by distinguishing senses of necessity: but he has a much richer panoply of distinctions than Grosseteste offers; the richest, indeed, of any medieval theologian I have studied on the topic.

11 BGPM, p. 165.

12 BGPM, p. 168.

13 Est necessarium duplex: uno modo, quod non habet posse aliquo modo ad eius oppositum vel cum initio vel fine, cuiusmodi est hoc: duo et tria esse quinque . . . Est et aliud necessarium, quod neque secundum praeteritum, neque secundum praesens, neque secundum futurum habet posse ad eius oppositum, sine tamen initio fuit posse ad hoc et fuit posse ad eius oppositum, et tale est antichristum fore futurum. BGPM pp. 168– 9.

14 BGPM, p. 173ff.

He sets out some of the distinctions in *De Universalibus* thus:

> We must make a distinction between kinds of necessity; there is absolute necessity, which cannot not be, and hypothetical necessity, based on an antecedent which is eternally the case.
>
> And that can be subdivided in accordance with types of truths; some of them last for ever, others last longer or shorter times according to the good pleasure of free will. For one kind of natural necessity is outside the necessitation of created free will, and another kind depends on that will. Again, one kind of necessity is the necessity of compulsion, when one person by compelling another necessitates him to cause some truth, and another kind is free necessity, free either in the sense of freedom between alternatives or of freedom from compulsion.[15]

In his textbook on logic Wyclif develops these distinctions in greater detail.[16] Absolute necessity comes in several kinds: two kinds are illustrated by the proposition 'God exists' on the one hand, and by the laws of geometry on the other. Laws of nature, as that a body will become hot in the presence of certain heating agents, sometimes seem to be described by Wyclif as cases of absolute necessity (the necessity of the hypothetical law) and sometimes as cases of conditioned or hypothetical necessity (the necessity of the event falling under the law). There are various types of hypothetical necessity, depending on whether the condition is an antecedent, a consequence, or an accompaniment of the conditioned event in question. The most important case is where

15 Hic oportet distingere de necessitate: quod quaedem est absoluta quae non potest non esse, alia autem est necessitas ex suppositione quam oportet esse ex antecedente aeterno. Et illud capit subdivisionem secundum naturas veritatum, ut alia est semper, alia diutius, vel brevius secundum beneplacitum libertatis. Alia enim est necessitas naturalis extra necessitationem creati liberi arbitrii, et alia dependet a tali arbitrio. Alia etiam est necessitas coactionis ut contingit cogentem alium necessitate ipsum ad causandum aliquam veritatem et alia est necessitas libera sive libertate contradictionis sive libertate a coactione. U, XIV, 54–66.

16 *Logice Continuacio* in *De Logica*, i, 75–234.

the condition is an antecedent; and this antecedent conditional necessity itself comes in three kinds.

One kind of such necessity is the necessity of volition: as when the unconstrained will of myself or of God is a cause which necessitates something else. Another is natural necessity, as when the application of fire in sufficient force to combustible material acts or begins to act. The third, the necessity of constraint, is the necessity by which a brigand compels his captive to purchase his ransom.[17]

Having laid out these distinctions, Wyclif can go on to treat the problem about foreknowledge and freedom which had been current since Grosseteste and his predecessors. He sets it out thus:

Every contingent truth is necessary according to the disposition of divine knowledge, even though many things are contingent between alternatives with respect to their secondary causes. For the following agrument is valid: God wills this to be, or knows it will be; therefore, at the appropriate time it is the case. The antecedent is eternally true with respect to any past or future effect. So in relation to the foreknowledge of God every effect is necessary to come about.[18]

Aristotle had said that everything which is, when it is, necessarily is. We must make the same judgement, Wyclif says, about what

17 Et est de necessitate antecedentis ulterius triplex subdivisio, cum aliqua sit talis necessitas volicionis: ut si volicio dei sit causa necessitans aliud non coacta; alia necessitas naturalis, ut necessitas qua ignis applicatus ad combustibile subdominans agit vel incipit agere; sed tercia, necessitas coaccionis, est necessitas qua predo cogit suum captivum ipsum redimere. *Logica Continuacio*, p. 158.

18 Omne verum contingens est necessarium secundum dispositionem divinae notionis, licet sint multa contingentia ad utrumlibet secundum causas secundas, nam sequitur: Deus vult vel scit hoc fore, ergo hoc est pro tempore suo. Antecedens est aeternaliter verum respectu cuiuscumque effectus praeteriti vel fururi. Ideo quoad praescientiam. Dei omnem effectum est necessarium evenire. U, XIV, 74–83.

will be and what has been. That is to say, what will be, will be necessary when it is. But is the future already necessary now?

> Once we have unravelled the ambiguity of 'necessity', it is clear how hypothetical necessity is consistent with supreme contingence. I do not mean sheerly hypothetical necessity, which does not posit either of the extremes, like 'if you are a donkey, you can be thwacked', because that is an absolutely necessary truth about the connection between the extremes. What I mean is an eternal contingent truth, entailing a truth occurring at a particular time, in such a way that the truth about the connection is absolutely necessary but the truth of the causal antecedent is contingent.[19]

What Wyclif means is this. We have the following valid argument:

1　If God has always known that John will sin today, John will sin today.
2　God has always known that John will sin today.
3　Therefore, John will sin today.

The first proposition is absolutely necessary, an eternal truth about the relationship between the other two propositions. But the second proposition, though it is a sempiternal truth, a truth which has always been true, is not a necessary truth, but a contingent truth.

But how can there be contingent truths about God? Surely, if something is contingent it can cease to be the case, and God is unchangeable. Wyclif's answer to this is similar to Grosseteste's: 'Although God can utterly contingently will or not will a given

---

19 Patet, detecta aequivocatione necessitatis, quomodo cum summa contingentia stat conditionata necessitas. Non autem intelligo necessitatem pure conditionatam quae non ponit alterum extremorum qualis est ista: si tu es asinus, tu es rudibilis, quia illa est veritas connexionis absolute necessaria, sed veritatem contingentem aeternam, inferentem veritatem temporaliter accidentem sic quod veritas connexionis est absolute necessaria, sed veritas antecedentis causantis est contingens. U, XIV, 98– 108.

object to volition, he cannot begin or cease actually to will, and thus he cannot change from volition to non-volition or *vice-versa*.[20]

God cannot change from knowing that p to knowing that not p, or from willing p to be the case to not willing p to be the case; but when he knows that p is the case, sometimes – in the cases where p is a contingent truth – it would have been possible that from all eternity he knew that not-p was the case. If this seems difficult to grasp, Wyclif reminds us that even in human affairs it is often possible for p's being the case to be something that depends on a free action of mine, and yet there never being a time when I can alter the truth-value of p. Thus, suppose it is true of me that I shall have a son. The coming true of this truth will depend, among other things, on free actions of mine. Yet at no time do I have the power to alter the truth-value of the proposition 'I will have a son'. For if it is true of me now, it was true at the moment of my birth. Similarly, though the truth of any contingent truth in the universe depends, among other things, on God's volitions, there was no time at which God had the power to change those volitions or to alter the truth-value of the contingent truths.[21]

Altogether, it seems that we can extract from Wyclif's writing nine different kinds of necessity, or nine different contrasts between necessity and contingency. To my knowledge, Wyclif never lists them all together, but a list may be useful, with some non-Wycliffian names for the different kinds.

1 There is the necessity illustrated by the truths of logic and geometry, which we may call logical necessity.
2 There is the natural necessity illustrated by the proposition that fire heats or by the laws of motion.
3 There are the eternal truths which concern not God's nature but his free decrees, e.g. 'God wills Wyclif to die in 1384'.
4 There are the sempiternal truths which are true at all times, though not through all eternity, e.g. 'the world exists', if we assume that there are only times while there is a world.

20 Quamvis Deus potest contingentissme velle et non velle datum volubile, non tamen potest incipere vel desinere ipsum velle et sic non potest mutari de volutione in non-volutionem vel econtra. U, XIV, 122–6.
21 U, XIV, 126–39.

5 There are inevitable truths, truths whose coming true is beyond the power of any created agent to prevent: e.g. 'the sun will rise tomorrow'.

6 There are immutable truths, truths which cannot be turned into falsehood: e.g. 'I have had a son'.

7 There is the necessity in human affairs which results from duress: e.g. we have no choice but to pay the kidnappers' ransom.

8 There are actions which are performed not under duress but spontaneously, and which yet cannot be helped: e.g. the blessed in heaven cannot help loving God.

9 Finally there are those actions which are performed with 'liberty of contradiction', i.e. when one has the power to do otherwise.

The necessity which contrasts with this last is the absence of alternative possibility. It is this kind of necessity which is the one most relevant to discussions of freedom and determinism.

Once the different kinds of necessity have been sorted out, it is clear that an event or a proposition can be necessary in one of these senses while being contingent in one or more of the other senses. In the passage most recently quoted Wyclif lays most strength on the distinction between necessary truths of the first two kinds, and the necessary truths of the third kind which are eternal truths which are contingent in the first and second senses, being neither truths of logic nor natural laws. This distinction is well taken. But does it avoid the problem of divine determinism? On Wyclif's own account, no secondary cause such as a human agent can act except in so far as it is directed to do so by a first cause which is God. Does not this destroy freedom? In reply, Wyclif makes two points: no created cause can necessitate a free agent; and though God can necessitate a human agent, he cannot compel or constrain him.

Although secondary causes can incline the created will to its proper act, neither they nor God can immediately compel it to the same, because, since the proper act of the will is willing, it is clear that it involves a contradiction that someone should perform such an act except willingly. However, God neces-

sitates to good willing, and permits man to necessitate himself
and subject himself to inferior creatures.[22]

Here the distinction between the seventh, eighth and ninth kinds of
necessity comes into play.

> To necessitate is one thing, and to compel another. Compul-
> sion is attributed to external or internal activity, when will is
> in some manner reluctant. Such necessity does not remove the
> desert of the will, any more than it takes away the freedom to
> act; though it quite properly rules out the supremely free
> action which is God's special prerogative. It is possible for a
> child to walk freely, though necessitated to walk as he does by
> his tutor leading him by the hand; similarly it is possible for
> the created will to be led by the spirit of God. But man has the
> freedom to walk away from the saving guidance on the
> disobedient feet of pride. Thus therefore, in both the inner act
> and the outer deed, there is contingent liberty and conditional
> necessity, but in the inborn intrinsic causation there is natural
> necessity.[23]

Wyclif's analogies are unconvincing, and it is hard to see how the
distinction between necessitating and permitting is to apply in the

22 Licet causae secundae inclinare possunt voluntatem creatam ad
actum proprium, tamen nec ipsae nec Deus possunt immediate cogere ad
eundem, quia, cum proprius actus voluntatis sit volutio, patet quod
claudit contradictionem ut aliquis ipsum eliciat nisi volens. Verumtamen
Deus necessitat ad benevolendum et permittit hominem necessitare se
ipsum et subicere se creaturae inferior. U, XIV, 256–64.

23 Aliud est autem necessitare et aliud cogere, cum coacrio dicitur
respectu operis extrinseci vel intrinseci, voluntate quoddamodo reclinante.
Nec tollit talis necessitas voluntatis meritum, sicut non tollit actum
liberum, licer decenter excludat actum liberrimum quod est Deo
specialiter reservatum. Sicut enim stat parvulum libere progredi dum
tamen necessitatus est sic progredi a pedagogo ducente, sic stat
voluntatem creatam, a spiritu Dei ductam. Homo tamen habet libertatem
exeundi a tali salutari regimine per inoboedientem pedem superbiae. Sic
ergo quantum ad actum elicitum et opus extrinsecum est contingens
libertas et conditionalis necessitas, sed quoad causationem innatam
intrinsecam est naturalis necessitas. U, XIV, 27–87.

case of God. The baby's steps are free only because the nurse cannot make him walk, but only guide him where to go; there is a distinction between what one human makes another do, and what he permits him to do, only because human beings have an independence of each other which no creature has of God. If what I do is entailed by ideas and volitions in the mind of God, how can I have any real power to determine my own action?

Wyclif puts this difficulty to himself very forcibly in the next section of the treatise, where he presents the following counter-argument to his thesis.

> It is necessary that particular events come about by absolute necessity, for God necessarily and independently fore-ordains, foresees, and wills, by the will of his good pleasure, every particular creature. Nothing can resist his will, and so nothing can prevent any effect. Just as no one can prevent the world's having been, no one can prevent any effect coming to be at the appropriate time. For the following argument is valid: God ordains this; therefore this will necessarily come to pass at the appropriate time. The antecedent is outside any created power and is accordingly altogether unpreventable. There-fore, so is everything which formally follows from it.[24]

In face of this objection. Wyclif reaffirms the crucial importance of human freedom: not just freedom from compulsion, but genuine freedom to choose between different alternatives.

> Many effects are within rational creatures' free power between alternatives, in such a way that they can make them to be and

---

24 Replicatur quod oportet de necessitate absoluta singula provenire, nam Deus necessario et independenter praeordinat, praescit, et vult voluntate beneplaciti singulas creaturas. Nec aliquid potest voluntati suae resistere, ergo nec effectum aliquem impedire. Sicut ergo nemo potest impedire quin mundus fuit sic nec aliquem effectum tempore suo fore. Sequitur enim: Deus ordinat hoc: ergo hoc necessario tempore suo erit. Antecedens est extra omnem potestatem creatam et per consequens omnino inimpedibile. Ergo et quodlibet formaliter inde sequens. U, XIV, 294–305. (I read *inimpedibile*, not *impedibile* as Mueller).

make them not to be; otherwise merit and demerit would be eliminated.[25]

How are we to reconcile this with the divine control over human actions? Wyclif's proposed solution is that we should say that the relationship between the divine volition and the human action is a two-way one: if God's volition causes man's act, so, in a sense, man's act causes God's volition. It is in the power of man to bring about, in respect of any of the eternal volitions in God, that none of them will be, and similarly with his non-volitions and *vice-versa*.

> On this it is to be noted that the volition of God, with respect to the existence of a creature, can be understood as a relationship, a mental entity with its basis in God's willing the thing to be according to its mental being – which is something absolutely necessary – and with its terminus in the existence of the creature in its own kind. And such a relationship depends on each of the terms, since if God is to will that Peter or some other creature should be it is requisite that it should in fact be. And thus the existence of the creature, even though it is temporal, causes in God an eternal mental relationship, which is always in process of being caused, and yet is always completely caused. Nor does it follow from this that God is changeable, since such a relationship is not the terminus of any change . . . nor does it follow from this that man can perfect God, or compel him, or cause in him volition, knowledge, or anything absolute.[26]

25 Multi effectus sunt in libera potestae contradictionis rationalis creaturae sic quod potest facere ipsos fore et potest facere quod non erunt, quia aliter tolleretur meritum atque demeritum. U, XIV, 322–25.

26 Pro quo notandum quod volutio Dei, respectu existentiae creaturae, potest intelligi secundum habitudinem relativam, ut est res rationis fundata in Deo volente rem esse secundum esse intelligibile – quod est absolute necessarium – et terminata ad existentiam creaturae in proprio genere. Et talis habitudo dependet ab utroque extremo, cum ad hoc quod Deus velit Petrum vel aliud factibile esse requiritur ipsum esse. Et ita existentia creaturae, licet sit temporalis, causat in Deo relationem rationis aeternam, quae semper causatur et semper est complete causata. Nec sequitur ex isto quod Deus sit mobilis, cum ad talem habitudinem non est

Thus, when God wills Peter to repent of his sin, it is true both to say that Peter is repenting because God wills him to repent, and that God wills him to repent because he is repenting. But God's eternal volition is a complex one, which includes other elements which in no way depend on Peter:

> So the proposition 'God wills Peter to grieve' reports many volitions in God, for instance, the volition by which he wills to be what is absolutely necessary, the volition by which he wills the specific nature to be, and this depends on no particular man, and the volition by which it pleases God that Peter grieves, which is one that depends on Peter's grief.[27]

In this way the objection that if God's ordaining is outside our power, then all that follows from his ordaining is outside our power, is answered in a dramatic fashion. Wyclif simply denies the antecedent: God's ordaining is not outside our power. God's eternal volition, he says, 'is not completely caused before the termination of the effect, although it is determinately and non-disjunctively true'.

Does this mean, that when I prevent something happening I prevent God from willing? That would be absurd. 'When I prevent a creature I do not prevent God from willing, since according to his decree from all eternity he never willed the prevented creature so to act.' But it is true that this eternal willing of God's is something that I bring about.[28]

There is no necessary principle to the effect that if I can prevent an antecedent from coming to pass, I can prevent a consequent from coming to pass. What is true is rather that if the antecedent is

---

motus . . . nec sequitur ex isto quod homo potest perficere Deum, cogere cum, vel causare in eo volutionem, scientiam vel aliquod absolutum. U, XIV, 328–44.

27 Haec ergo propositio 'Deus vult Petrum dolere' dicit quotlibet volutiones in Deo, ut puta volutionem qua vult hoc esse quod est absolute necessarium, volutionem qua vult naturam specificam esse et hoc a nullo singulari homine dependet, et volutionem qua placet Deo quod Petrus doleat. Et illa dependet a dolore Petri. U, XIV, 346–52.

28 U, XIC, I 386–99.

something altogether outside my power, to bring about or bring about its contradictory, then anything logically following from it is equally firmly so.

Wyclif sums up the relations between necessity and contingency:

> All future things will come to pass necessarily by hypothetical necessity, and yet will come to pass most contingently. Similarly, the truths which thus necessitate them came to pass necessarily, and yet it can be the case that they did not. Indeed you can make it be the case that they did not, and yet you cannot make them cease to be, nor can you make what has been begotten not have been begotten . . . All these and similar things are obvious from the infallible principle that with God all things which ever have been or will ever be are present, and thus, if something has been or will be, it is at the appropriate time. Blessed, then, be the Lord of time, who has lifted us above time to see that magnificent truth.[29]

Wyclif ends chapter fourteen of *De Universalibus* with a discussion of the proposition that there is everywhere absolute necessity (the proposition, roughly, for which he was later posthumously condemned at Constance). He will have no truck with it.

> To maintain this position is contrary to philosophy and to our Faith. It is contrary to philosophy, because if that were so nothing would happen contingently or by chance, but would come about by absolute necessity like the inward production of the Word. Nor would there be any moral virtue, since for those things which are not in our power we are neither to be

---

29 Omnia futura necessario – necessitate ex suppositione – sunt futura, quae tamen contingentissime sunt futura. Et sic veritates sic necessitantes necessario fuerunt, et tamen potest esse quod non fuerunt. Immo, tu potes facere quod non fuerunt et tamen non potes facere illa desinere fuisse vel commutare genitum in ingenitum . . . Omnia ista et eis similia patent ex hoc infallibili principio quod apud Deum sunt omnia, quae fuerunt vel erunt praesentia, et sic, si aliquid fuit vel erit, ipsum est pro suo tempore. Unde benedictus sit Dominus temporis, qui elevavit nos supra tempus ad videndum istam veritatem praeclaram. U, XIV, 409–24.

praised or blamed morally. According to this thesis it would be no more in the power of any creature to affect what a man might do than to prevent a star from rising or to prevent something being brought about by God; it is absolutely necessary for every effect to come about. The opposite truth is a self-evident one which must be dinned in by blows.[30]

To show that the proposition is against the Faith, Wyclif goes on to explain that it is incompatible with a number of well-known passages of Scripture.

We can see, then, how misleading it is to suggest that Wyclif went beyond contemporary theologians in limiting human freedom in the interests of divine omnipotence. On the contrary, he took the highly unusual step of safeguarding human freedom by extending its sphere of action to the eternal volitions of God himself. It cannot be claimed that Wyclif's solution resolves the problem. When he distinguishes God's decrees into complex relational volitions, one simply wants to restate the objection in terms of the absolute mental volitions which are one element of the complex, an element which seems quite beyond human control. But no other medieval theologian succeeded in giving a satisfactory answer to the antinomy of divine power and human freedom, and perhaps no satisfactory answer will ever be possible. Where Wyclif departs from his colleagues is not in imputing extra necessity to human actions, but in assigning unusual contingency to divine volitions.

30 Hic videtur mihi quod repugnat philosophiae et Fidei nostrae sic ponere. Philosophiae, quia sic nihil fieret contingenter sive fortuite, cum fieret absolute necessario, sicut Verbum ad intra producitur. Nec foret aliqua virtus moralis, cum propter illa quae non sunt in potestate nostra nec sumus laudandi nec culpandi moraliter. Sed secundum istam positionem non plus subiacet potestati creaturae declinare quicquid homo fecerit quam impedire ne astrum oriatur vel ne a Deo aliquid producatur, quia omnem effectum est absolute necessarium evenire. Ideo oppositum tamquam per se notum est per verbera inducendum. U, XIV, 456–68.

IV

Metaphysics, Morals and Politics

10

Abortion and the
Taking of Human Life

Abortion is a difficult topic for the moral philosopher. The difficulty is not just that strong views are held on both sides of the debate about the rightness or wrongness of abortion. The problem is that the issue of abortion is interlocked with several of the most difficult general problems in moral philosophy (the debate between absolutism and consequentialsim; the pros and cons of utilitarianism; the moral significance of the distinction between doing things and letting them happen) and with some of the most profound issues in metaphysics (the nature of life, the essence of human personality, the principle of individuation, the relationship between actuality and potentiality). To present a fully worked out moral theory of the ethics of abortion involves taking sides in a number of debates which have exercised philosophers for generations.

This is one reason why any judgement about abortion by a philosopher will be controversial. But the morality of abortion, though controversial, is not a borderline issue. There are a number of difficult and controversial issues – such as the morality of white lies, or certain forms of tax evasion, or the propriety of various kinds of social discrimination – where reasonable people may differ and arguments may be offered on both sides. But issues of this kind involve drawings of moral boundaries which both sides may agree to be to a certain extent arbitrary; and nobody thinks particularly ill of someone for taking the opposite side in this kind of debate. But it is different in the case of abortion: here we have an action which, if it is wrong at all, is very wrong indeed. Abortion is not the only such instance: the morality of nuclear deterrence provides a similar case.

Considered moral judgement about abortion is made more difficult still when the issue is presented within the context of feminism. Abortion is sometimes treated as a moral issue within the exclusive competence of women: as the women's issue *par excellence*. It is absurd to suggest that only women are in a position to make moral judgements about abortion; there is no moral issue which falls within the exclusive domain of either sex, for men and women belong to the same human moral community, and if they did not the issue of fairness between men and women could never arise. But one does not have to be a feminist to accept that the issue of abortion is of quite special concern to women. For while, if abortion is held permissible, those who suffer from it will be divided roughly equally between members of either gender, if abortion is prohibited, the burdens resulting from the prohibition lie much more heavily upon the female sex than on the male.

Many opponents of abortion see the issue as essentially a simple one. Their argument can be summed up in a nutshell: Taking innocent human life is always wrong. Abortion is taking innocent human life. Therefore, abortion is always wrong. I believe that this argument is essentially correct; but I do not think that it is at all as simple a matter as it appears. There are many ways in which the two premises of the argument can be attacked, and in order to show that the attacks fail, the premises need to be spelt out, explained, and to a certain extent qualified. This I shall now try to do; and while I hope that the explications which I will offer will bring out the essential soundness of the anti-abortionist position, I must expect that some of the qualifications I shall introduce may well be unwelcome to many of those who oppose abortion.

The first premise of the argument against abortion is the proposition that taking innocent human life is always wrong. This proposition is also the starting point of many of the arguments offered by those who oppose nuclear warfare and the mass-bombing of cities. Those who affirm the proposition do not normally wish to rule out any action whatsoever which may result in the death of the innocent: in the context of warfare, it will be allowed, it may be legitimate to attack military targets even though some civilian deaths may unintentionally result; similarly, moralists and divines have long agreed that a pregnant woman in illness may be offered necessary medication even if it is foreseen that an abortion may ensue. What the proposition is meant to rule out is the intentional killing of the innocent: killing that is directly intentional in the sense that the death of the innocent human being is either an end of the agent or a means to one of his ends.

Many contemporary moral philosophers would reject the proposition that taking innocent human life is always wrong. It is not common to find moralists who believe that while there are some actions which are always wrong, killing the innocent is not one of them. What is widespread is rather the view that there are no actions which are always wrong; that there are no kinds of action which must be avoided, come what may, whatever the circumstances or consequences of avoiding them. Moralists of this school of thought are often called *consequentialists*, since they believe that the morality of an action should be judged by its consequences. Moralists who believe that there are some actions, such as taking innocent life, which should never be performed are called, by contrast, *absolutist*.

An absolutist, then, in this sense, is one who believes that there are some kinds of actions which should never be done, no matter what the consequences are of refraining from doing them. The consequentialist with whom he is contrasted believes that there is no category of act which may not, in special circumstances, be justified by its consequences.

The distinction between absolutist and consequentialist should not be confused with the distinction between absolutist and relativist. In the sense of this second contrast, an absolutist is a person who thinks that there are some moral principles which are valid for all human beings; a relativist thinks that moral principles hold only within particular societies, or at particular times.

Most absolutists are no doubt absolutists in both senses. But the two contrasts are quite distinct. Let us call an absolutist in contrast to a consequentialist a *prohibitionist*: he is an absolutist in that he believes some things are absolutely prohibited. Let us call an absolutist who is contrasted with a relativist a *universalist*: he is an absolutist because he thinks there are some principles which are absolutely universal, no matter what the time or place.

One can be a universalist without being a prohibitionist. Classical utilitarians like Bentham were consequentialists, but the principle of utility – the greatest happiness of the greatest number – was as valid in the twelfth century as the eighteenth, in Hanoi as in Hampstead. One can be a prohibitionist without being a universalist. One may subscribe to the principle in our society that nothing will ever justify infanticide, while thinking that in other societies it may be permissible. For purposes of practical debate about abortion, and abortion legislation, in countries such as the UK and the US is it not conflict between universalism and relativism that matters, but the issue between prohibitionism and consequentialism.

Thoroughgoing consequentialism is probably more popular in theory than in practice: outside philosophy seminars perhaps not many people will agree that no kind of action, however outrageous, can be morally ruled out in advance, and that one should literally stop at nothing in the pursuit of desirable consequences. But there is, equally, a very widespread suspicion of prohibitionism. Two objections to prohibitionism are particularly common.

First, do not absolute prohibitions often lead to absurd, morally repugant, conclusions? To take a fictional case much discussed by moral philosophers: suppose that a corpulent schoolmaster takes a group of twenty pupils potholing, and on the way back to the upper air gets stuck in the exit; he cannot be pushed one way or the other, and if he stays where he is the twenty pupils will die for lack of oxygen. Surely here it would be right to blow up the fat teacher to save the twenty trapped children? But to do so would be to violate the prohibition on killing the innocent.

Secondly, where do these absolute prohibitions come from? No doubt religious believers see them as coming from God; but how are they to convince unbelievers of this, and if they cannot how can they expect unbelievers to feel bound by them? Surely only someone who believes in God, and indeed in a specific divine revelation, can consistently uphold the notion that some acts are absolutely prohibited. Can there be a prohibition without a prohibiter? Does not someone who subscribes to absolute prohibitions merely express the prejudices of his upbringing?

In my view, these objections show a misunderstanding of what morality is. There appear to be three elements which are essential to morality: a moral community; a set of moral values; and a moral code. All three are necessary. First, it is as impossible to have a purely private morality as it is to have a purely private language, and for very similar reasons. Secondly, the moral life of the community consists in the shared pursuit of non-material values such as fairness, truth, comradeship, freedom: it is this which distinguishes between morality and economics. Thirdly, this pursuit is carried out within a framework which excludes certain types of behaviour: it is this which marks the distinction between morality and aesthetics.

If this is correct, then prohibitionism is not simply one form of morality, not just a preferred form: it is something constitutive of morality as such. The answer to the question 'Who does the prohibiting?' is that it is the members of the moral community who do it: membership of a common moral society involves subscription to a common code. Universalism, as defined above, can now be seen to be the belief that any member of any moral community belongs to the single community which is the human race: that is, that there are moral relationships, and shared values and codes, between any two human beings.

To give a less schematic answer to the question 'Where do moral codes come from?' one must make distinctions. The question may be historical or epistemological. Historically, the answer is that each person acquires a moral code from the society in which she is brought up; she may, and commonly will, criticize and reject some part of it. Epistemologically, the answer is that moral codes are justified and criticized in terms of their effects on the moral values of the community. Indirectly, they are also criticized or justified in terms of material values, since moral values are often second-order values concerning the distribution of non-moral goods and evils, benefits and burdens.

There is no general principle from which moral principles can be derived, as theorems from an axiom; equally, there is no one source – e.g. sense-data – from which all our non-moral knowledge is derived. The moral and non-moral values which provide the justification for moral codes are various and independent of each other.

Moreover what is justified is not the individual act in accordance with the principles of the code. It is by reference to the effect of the principle – in general – to these values that its merit is assessed. It may well be that a particular act or omission, in accordance with a moral code, will not be deleterious to a particular value of the society. And yet it may be conducive to the society's values that this kind of act be prohibited.

It is thus that the absolutist (prohibitionist) answers the difficult cases brought against her by the consequentalist – such as the trapped potholer conundrum. Innocent life is more secure in a society in which the code forbids the killing of the innocent in general, even though in individual cases innocent lives may be lost as a result of the observance of the code.

Not all those who oppose abortion are prohibitionists. Similarly, there are many who oppose nuclear deterrence on grounds which are utilitarian rather than absolutist. But so many of those who believe that abortion is wrong do so on the grounds that it is something that is absolutely prohibited, that it seemed worthwhile to spell out, and defend, the kind of absolutism involved.

Let us turn to the second premise of the anti-abortion argument: abortion is taking innocent human life. Defenders of abortion will dispute this, saying that a foetus is not yet a human being, even though it will become one. Until comparatively recent times theologians who condemned abortion none the less agreed with the proposition that a foetus was not yet a human being, at least in the early stages of pregnancy; they condemned abortion not as the destruction, but as the prevention, of the life of a human being. Their judgement on this matter was based on superannuated biology; but the question remains a contentious one, whether a foetus is a human being, and if so at what stage of its development it begins to be one.

The question is often posed in the confused form: 'When does life begin?'. If this means 'At what stage of the process between conception and birth are we dealing with living matter?' the answer is obvious: at every stage. At fertilization egg and sperm unite to form a single cell: that is a living cell, just as the egg and the sperm were themselves alive before their fusion. But this is clearly not the question which is relevant to the moral issue of abortion: worms and rosebuds are equally indubitably alive, but no one seeks to give their lives the protection of the law. So perhaps we reformulate the question 'When does human life begin?'. Here too the answer is obvious but inadequate: the newly formed conceptus is a *human* conceptus, not a canine or leonine one; so in that sense its life is a human life. But equally the sperm and ovum from which the conceptus originated were human sperm and human ovum; but no one wishes to describe them as human beings or unborn children. If asked 'When does life begin?' we must respond with another question 'When does the life *of what* begin?'.

Sometimes the question is formulated not in terms of life, but in terms of animation or personhood. Thus, we ask 'When does the soul enter the body?' or 'When does an embryo become a human person?'. Contemporary discussions of the morality of abortion and the status of the foetus often shy away from these questions. Thus, in the Commons debate on Mr Enoch Powell's *Unborn Children (Protection) Bill* (15 February 1985, *Hansard*, vol. 73, col. 651) Mr St John Stevas said:

> We need not bother ourselves about recondite questions of when the soul, if there be a soul, enters the body. That is a theological question. It does not provide the opportunity for a final answer. Nor need we, in my opinion, discuss when a human personality is present in an embryo. Again, that is a metaphysical question.

The Warnock Committee, whose report on human fertilization and embryology (Cmnd. 9314) was the occasion for Mr Powell's bill, had similarly attempted to short circuit the question of personhood. Some people, the committee observed, think that if it could be decided when an embryo becomes a person, it could also be decided when it might, or might not, be permissible for scientific research to be undertaken upon embryos. The committee did not agree.

Although the questions of when life or personhood begin appear to be questions of fact susceptible of straight-forward answers, we hold that the answers to such questions in fact are complex amalgams of factual and moral judgements. Instead of trying to answer these questions directly we have therefore gone straight to the question of *how it is right to treat the human embryo.*

A philosopher writing on these matters cannot evade, as a politician or a committee may do, the question of personhood. It is indeed a metaphysical question when personhood begins: that does not mean that it is an unanswerable question, but that it is a question for the metaphysician to answer. The question about personhood is also the same as the question about life, rightly understood. For 'When does life begin?' must mean 'When does the life of the individual person begin?'.

The question is a philosophical one, but in order to answer it one does not need to introduce philosophical jargon, or appeal to quasi-theological concepts such as the soul. As so often in philosophical perplexity what is needed is not recondite information, or technical concepts, but reflection on truths which are obvious and for that reason easily overlooked.

If a mother looks at her daughter, six months off her twenty-first birthday, she can say to her with truth 'If I had had an abortion twenty-one years ago today, I would have killed you'. Each of us, looking back to the date of our birthday, can say with truth 'If my mother had had an abortion six months before that date, I would have been killed'. Truths of this kind are obvious, and can be formulated without any philosophical technicality, and involve no smuggled moral judgements.

Taking this as our starting point, however, it is easier to find our way through the moral maze. Those who defend abortion on the grounds that foetuses are not human beings or human persons are arguing, in effect, that they are not members of the same moral community as adult humans. But truths of the kind which we have just illustrated show that foetuses are identical with the adult humans which are the prime examples of members of the moral community.

It is true that a foetus cannot yet engage in moral thinking or the rational judgement of action which enables adults to interrelate morally with each other. But neither can a young child or baby, and we do not think this temporary inability gives us the right to take the life of a child or baby. It is the long-term capacity for rationality which makes us accord to the child the same moral protection as the adult, and which should make us accord the like respect to whatever has the same long-term capacity, even before birth.

To be sure, there can be goodness or badness in human actions with regard to beings that are not members of the human moral community. Those who believe in God do not think of him as a member of our moral community, and yet regard humans as having a duty towards him of worship. Non-human animals are not part of our moral community, and yet it is wrong to be cruel to them. But the moral respect we accord to children and, if I am right, should accord to foetuses is something quite different to the circumspection proper in our relation with animals. For the individual which is now a foetus or a child, if all goes well, will take its place with us, as the animal never will, as an equal member of the moral community; as Kant might say, as a fellow-legislator in the kingdom of ends.

I have claimed it as an obvious truth that a foetus six months from term is the same individual as the human child and adult into which, in the natural course of events, it will grow after birth. This seems true in exactly the same sense as it is true that the child is the same individual as the adult into which it will grow, all being well, after adolescence. But if we trace the history of the individual backward towards conception, then matters cease to be similarly obvious.

It may be thought that there is something odd about the whole procedure of trying to settle the moral status of a foetus and an embryo by working backwards from a consideration of the adult and infant. But, as the Warnock Committee pointed out, this is the procedure the law finds natural.

Under civil law in England and Wales the *Congenital Disabilities (Civil Liability) Act 1976* allows, in limited circumstances, damages to be recovered where an embryo or foetus has been injured *in utero* through the negligence of some third person. It is thus accorded a kind of retrospective status where it is born deformed or damaged as a result of injury.

The retrospective procedure in such cases is only an extension before birth of the attitude we take towards children when we seek to protect them from disablements of all kinds including those which will only exhibit themselves in adult life.

But there are difficulties in tracing the history of an individual back from the foetal stage towards the moment of conception. Many opponents of abortion see no such difficulty. In the debate on the Powell bill, Sir Gerald Vaughan, opposing experimentation on embryos, had this to say:

> It is unarguable that at the point of fertilization something occurs which is not present in the sperm or the unfertilized ovum. What occurs is the potential for human life – not for life in general, but life for a specific person. That fertilized ovum carries the structure of a specific human being – the height, the colour, the colour of his or her eyes, and all the other details of a specific person. I do not think that there can be any argument against that. The fact that the embryo at that stage does not bear a human form seems to me to beg the issue and to be quite irrelevant. It carries the potential, and, just as the child is to the adult human, so the embryo must be to the child.

Sir Gerald concluded, following the Royal College of Nursing, that human rights were applicable to an embryo from the first moment of conception.

Sir Gerald obviously chose his words with care, and what he says about the potential for human life is absolutely correct: in the conceptus there is the blueprint for 'the structure of a specific human being'. But if he is to establish his conclusion, he needs a different premise, which is that the conceptus contains the structure of an individual human being. But a specific human being is not an individual human being. This is an instance of a very general point about the difference between specification and individuation. The general point is that nothing is ever individuated merely by a specification of its properties, however detailed or complete. It is always at least logically possible that there should be two or more individuals answering to the same specification; any blueprint may be used more than once. Two peas in a pod may be as alike as you please: what makes them two individuals rather than one is that they are two different parcels of matter, not necessarily that they differ in description. In the case of human beings the possibility of two individuals answering to the same specification is not just a logical possibility: it is a possibility which is realized in the case of identical twins. For this reason an embryo in the early days after fertilization cannot be regarded as an individual human being. The single cell after fusion is totipotential, in the sense that from it develop all the different tissues and organs of the human body, as well as the tissues that become the placenta. In its early days a single embryo may turn into something which is not a human being at all, or something which is one human being, or something which is two people or more.

For this reason, if a mother points to her child and says 'If the embryo in my fallopian tube nine months before your birth had been destroyed, you would have been destroyed' what she says is not an obvious truth parallel to those we illustrated earlier. We may, of course, say to one of our children 'You were conceived while we were on that holiday in Venice', and this is not simply a metaphorical utterance similar to 'All those years ago you were only a twinkle in your father's eye'. But it does not have the same kind of meaning as 'You would have been killed if I had had an abortion six months before the date of your birthday'. For there is not the uninterrupted history of a single individual linking conception with the present, as there is linking foetal life with the present life of the child or adult.

There is, indeed, an uninterrupted history of development linking conception with the present life of the adult; but there is equally an uninterrupted history of development back from the present to the origination of each of the gametes which fused at conception. But this is not the uninterrupted history of an individual. For each of the gametes might, in different circumstances, have fused to form a different conceptus; and the conceptus might, in different circumstances, have turned into more or less than the single individual which it did in fact turned into. Of course all development, if it is to proceed, depends on factors in the environment: an adult may die if diseased and a child may die if not nourished, just as an ovum will die if not fertilized and a conceptus will die if not implanted. But though children and adults may die, they cannot become part of something else or turn into someone else. Foetus, child and adult have a continuous *individual* development which gamete and embryo do not have.

At what point, or by what time, has an embryo become an individual human being? If we can answer that question, it seems that we can give a non-arbitrary date from which abortion becomes morally impermissible. The Warnock Committee was not considering the morality of abortion, but (*inter alia*) the morality of experimentation on embryos; but the deliberations of the committee are very relevant to the ethical issues surrounding abortion, though for political reasons many discussions of the Warnock report have played down this relevance. A minority of the Warnock Committee thought experimentation on embryos should be altogether prohibited; the majority were in favour of allowing it, but thought it should be impermissible after the fourteenth day. Their reasons for fixing this term were well summarized by the Minister of Health, Mr Kenneth Clarke, in his speech in the debate on Mr Powell's bill (col. 686)

A cell that will become a human being – an embryo or conceptus – will do so within fourteen days. If it is not implanted within fourteen days it will never have a birth. The majority of embryos do not implant. Nobody knows exactly how many . . .

The committee thought that experiments should be licensed as long as no embryo was kept alive for more than fourteen days *in vitro*. The basis for the fourteen day limit was that it related to the stage of implantation which I have just described, and to the stage at which it is still uncertain whether an embryo will divide into one or more individuals, and thus up to the stage before true individual development has begun. Up to fourteen days that embryo could become one person, two people, or even more . . . (Also) fourteen days is the stage before which the rudiments of the nervous system have been laid down . . . that means that as far as anyone can tell, pain does not enter into these experiments.

Many people seem to think that it is a decisive factor in assessing the morality of abortion whether or not the foetus feels pain in the process of abortion. The film *The Silent Scream* was made by opponents of abortion in the hope of convincing supporters of abortion that the foetus does indeed feel pain. But whether or not the foetus feels pain in an abortion, in an abortion it is undoubtedly deprived of life. Someone who thinks that it is permissible to kill a foetus but not permissible to cause it pain must think of it as like a non-human animal, which we have the right to kill provided we do so humanely without unnecessary suffering. But for someone who regards the foetus as a human being the issue of pain can be no more than marginal. Even with adult human beings, the wrongness of deliberately injuring them arises far more from the disablement caused by injury than from the pain involved in its infliction. And whereas death is not painful (even if dying is) death is total disablement: so there is an *a fortiori* argument from the wrongness of disablement to the wrongness of killing, where there is no *a fortiori* argument from the wrongness of causing pain to the wrongness of killing.

Mr Powell's bill to prohibit experimentation on embryos was supported, on a vote, by 238 MPs against 66. Critics of the bill pointed out that it was inconsistent for the House of Commons to prohibit the destruction of embryos at an inchoate stage while permitting the abortion of well-developed foetuses. Supporters of the Warnock Committee's proposals argued that it was inconsistant for critics to object to the destruction of embryos by experimentation while permitting their destruction by intra-uterine contraceptive devices.

Both points seem to me well taken. The use of the intra-uterine coil is not, as is sometimes said, a form of abortion. That is because what is destroyed is not a human individual as a developed foetus is. On the other hand, all the reasons put forward by the Warnock

Committee for prohibiting experimentation on embryos after the fourteenth day seem to be equally good reasons for prohibiting the destruction of embryos and the abortion of foetuses after that day also.

A foetus, while being a human individual, is of course also uniquely involved with the life of another human individual, namely the woman in whose womb it is implanted. Because the life of the two are so closely interwoven, the recognition of the general wrongness of abortion does not settle the question – a difficult one which I do not attempt to investigate here – of the correct moral decision in cases where the foetus presents a threat to the physical life of the mother in which it is developing. There are two extreme positions in this area: the feminist view that the foetus should be regarded simply as a part of the mother's body like any of her own organs, on the one hand, and the view common among Catholic theologians that the foetus should never be aborted even if the only alternative is the death of both mother and foetus. Both positions seem to me clearly wrong, but it is not easy to state exactly where the truth lies between these two extremes.

Before the debate on the *Unborn Children Bill* Mr St John-Stevas presented a petition, bearing two million signatures, which began: 'The Humble Petition of the residents of the United Kingdom of Great Britain and Northern Ireland showeth that we affirm that the newly fertilized human embryo is a real, living individual human being.' There may be good reason for prohibiting experimentation on embryos, as the petitioners prayed. But this affirmation, if the argument of this paper has been correct, is not justified. The newly fertilized embryo is indeed real, living and human: but it is not an *individual* human being.

No doubt, in arguing for the general wrongness of abortion, I would find company among the great majority of the signatories to the St John-Stevas petition. But if the moral objection to abortion is to be coherently stated, I believe, abortion must be carefully defined. The correct way to state the objection to abortion is this: In so far as abortion is the termination of the life *of an actual, identifiable human individual* it is wrong.

11

Religion, Church and State in History and Philosophy

The question has been long debated whether the propagation of religious truth is one of the ends of civil government. In most countries of the West that question would now be answered in the negative. The question is not the same as the question whether the temporal welfare of human beings is more important than their spiritual welfare. One can agree that spiritual interests are paramount over material interests, and yet say that the functions of civil government are temporal and not spiritual. The institutions of religion have one purpose, and the institutions of the state have another, and the two should be kept separate, whatever the relative importance of the two.

This point was made vividly in the last century by Lord Macaulay in his essay 'Gladstone on church and state':[1]

> Without a division of labour the world could not go on. It is of very much more importance that men should have food than that they should have pianofortes. Yet it by no means follows that every pianoforte maker should add the business of a baker to his own; for, if he did so, we should have both much worse music and much worse bread ... The community would be thrown into universal confusion, if it were supposed to be the duty of every association which is formed for one good object to promote every other good object.

1 References are given to the Oxford edition of 1923.

What are the good objects for which civil government is instituted? There is disagreement, in the twentieth century as in the nineteenth, about the extent to which government should control and direct the activities of citizens; but there would be wide and almost universal agreement about some of the minimum and essential functions of government. The role of government is to protect the persons of citizens from injury and attack, to enable citizens peacefully to enjoy the use of material goods according to the property conventions of the society, to provide systems of arbitration to enable citizens to settle their disputes without resort to main force; to provide, directly or indirectly, institutions for the construction of works and the provision of goods which are beyond the powers of citizens as individuals or families: works such as roads and bridges, goods such as education and health care. It is, I claim, the role of government to provide these 'directly or indirectly': it is a matter of continuing dispute whether in these matters a government does better to act directly (by setting up a state system of transport, education, health service) or indirectly (by legislating in such a way as to enable and encourage private associations to furnish these goods).

The role of religious institutions differs from the role of civil government. The precise role of these institutions would be stated differently within different religious traditions: but as a rough and ready generalization it might be said that religious institutions exist for the propagation of religious belief, the promotion of spiritual welfare, and the provision for the worship of the divine. These purposes are clearly distinct from those of civil government as just described. But if one grants – as I have just granted, and as a nineteenth-century liberal might not have granted – that the provision of education and the custody of health can be legitimate concerns of civil government, why not also the promotion of religion?

There are two arguments which are commonly put forward in liberal societies for making a distinction here. For the first, let Macaulay again act as spokesman. The primary objects of civil government, he argues, are things which any human being, without reference to any higher power, or any future state, is very deeply interested.

Every human being, be he idolater, Mohammedan, Jew, Papist, Socinian, Deist or Atheist, naturally loves life, shrinks from pain, desires comforts which can be enjoyed only in communities where property is secure. To be murdered, to be tortured, to be robbed, to be sold into slavery, these are evidently evils from which men of every religion, and men of no religion, wish to be protected; and therefore it will hardly be disputed that men of every religion, and of no religion, have thus far a common interest in being well governed. (p. 341)

But there is not similar agreement when we turn from the ends of civil government to the ends of religious institutions. Macaulay is prepared to grant that in all ages and nations men of all orders of intellect have believed in the existence of some superior mind.

But whether there be one God, or many, what may be God's natual and what his moral attributes, in what relation His creatures stand to Him, whether He have ever disclosed Himself to us by any other revelation than that which is written in all the parts of the glorious and well ordered world which He had made, whether his revelation be contained in any permanent record, how that record should be interpreted, and whether it have pleased him to appoint any unerring interpreter on earth, these are questions respecting which there exists the widest diversity of opinion, and respecting some of which a large part of our race has, ever since the dawn of regular history, been deplorably in error. (p. 342)

The disagreement, then, among human beings about the nature of religious truth is one argument that is used against allotting, as a task to government, its propagation. Another argument is often put forward: religious values, unlike the security of persons and property, cannot be promoted by coercion. It does not matter, the argument goes, whether life is preserved and property protected out of benevolence or out of fear of the consequences of breaking the law. But worship which is enforced by the threat of worldly punishment cannot be pleasing to God in the way that the service of a willing heart is pleasing to him.

Despite these two arguments, throughout the history of the world governments have endeavoured to enforce religious belief and practice. This has been so, most obviously, in theocratic societies in which the promotion of a particular religion has been explicitly seen as one of the major tasks of government, and in which the heads of State have been allotted a special role within Churches, and the governmental and ecclesiastical hierarchies have been, if not identical, interwoven. Such was the condition of much of Europe throughout the medieval and early modern period. Though, in Christian Europe, a distinction was drawn between the role of the Church in declaring an offender to be a heretic, and the role of the secular power in executing him by burning, both powers regarded the preservation of orthodoxy as being one of the main purposes of their joint endeavour. As late as the sixteenth century, lay politicians as enlightened as Sir Thomas More would defend the persecution of heretics as something essential, not only to the preservation of true religion, but also to the cohesion of civil society itself. And as late as the nineteenth century, Mr Gladstone would defend the imposition of a particular religion – the Protestant religion – upon an unwilling population – the population of Ireland. 'We believe' he wrote 'that that which we place before them is, whether they know it or not, calculated to be beneficial to them; and that, if they know it not now, they will know it when it is presented to them fairly. Shall we, then, purchase their applause at the expense of their substantial, nay their spiritual interests?' (Quoted by Macaulay, p. 366)

Against this view, Macaulay insisted on the liberal position: that it was no part of the primary role of government to promote religion.

> We think that government, like every other contrivance of human wisdom, from the highest to the lowest, is likely to answer to its main end best when it is constructed with a single view to that end . . . A blade which is designed both to shave and to carve will certainly not shave so well as a razor, or carve so well as a carving-knife. An academy of painting, which should also be a bank, would, in all probability, exhibit very bad pictures and discount very bad bills. On this

principle we think that government should be organized solely with a view to its main end; and that no part of its efficiency for that end should be sacrificed in order to promote any other end however excellent. (p. 386)

Of course, it did not follow that governments should not pursue any ends other than their main end: government could encourage fine arts, improve steam navigation, ensure that the citizens were well educated. It could indeed, take an interest in religious instruction, provided that were done as a secondary end and in ways which did not conflict with the primary end. But no promotion of religion which contravened the primary end was justifiable. Thus:

All persecution directed against the persons or property of men is, on our principle, obviously indefensible. For, the protection of the persons and property of men being the primary end of government, and religious instruction only a secondary end, to secure the people from heresy by making their lives, their limbs, or their estates insecure would be to sacrifice the primary end to the secondary end. So too, would any civil disabilities on ground of religious opinion: for they would make government less efficient by depriving it of the service of able men and women. (p. 389)

In most countries in the Western world the last century has seen the effective triumph of the liberal system. Few states with a Christian religious tradition now see it as part of the role of the State to impose or propagate any form of the Christian tradition. This is so not only in countries like the United States where there is, under the First Amendment, official separation of Church and State, but also in Britain where one form of Christianity is an established Church, and even in countries like the Republic of Ireland where the overwhelming majority of the population consists of Roman Catholics and where the constitution bears the marks of Catholic political theory. In countries such as Ireland and Italy the issue is blurred somewhat because of attempts by Catholics to use the state to enforce doctrines (such as the wrongness of divorce or abortion) which according to Catholic belief are part of the natural law, obligations imposed by God on all human beings. From the outside, of course, this appears indistinguishable from attempts to use the apparatus of state institutions to impose Catholic belief; but it remains true that Catholics do not claim that it is right to enforce specifically Catholic practices (such as fasts or the attendance at Mass on Sundays) upon unwilling citizens; and more and more Catholics, while continuing to believe that divorce, contraception, and abortion are immoral for everyone and not just for Catholics, regard it as wrong to impose this morality on citizens – whether Catholic or not – by the coercive power of the civil authority.

In general, in Western countries at the present time, when disputes break out over the lines of demarcation between Church and State the question is commonly raised not by the intervention of the State in matters belonging to the Church, but by the intervention of the Church in issues pertaining to the State. There are still, of course, many areas where the regulation of the relationships between members of different religions is one of the most important functions of the State, and where the rivalry between different religious groups is the most potent source of civil disorder. It is not hard to think of tragic examples, whether the warring groups are different sects of Christians (as in Northern Ireland) or whether the conflict is between Christians and members of other faiths (as in Cyprus and Lebanon). But the conflicts here have not arisen from attempts by government to impose one religion on citizens in despite of another; on the contrary, the constitutional arrangements have been designed to prevent the unfair domination of one religious group by another, and the conflicts have arisen because of the breakdown or inefficacy of the civil power to act as a neutral arbiter between the opposing religious factions.

The high-water mark of the tide of liberalism, of the separation between Church and State, came in the later years of the nineteenth century and the early years of the twentieth. In Western Europe, liberal republics or constitutional monarchies had supplanted theocratic states and hieratic kingdoms. The secular German Empire of Bismarck had replaced the Holy Roman Empire and the Teutonic monk-knights. Where once the Pope had ruled, the liberal Savoyard monarchy held sway. The Empires of

Western powers in other continents provided, it is true, fertile fields for Christian missionaries; but the imperial powers in general held these missionaries at arm's length and allowed them no power in imperial administration; and with regard to the indigenous religious traditions, the imperial administrators saw it as one of the most important of their tasks to moderate religious passion and to keep the peace between hostile sects. The overarching theory was that Church and State had distinct spheres which did not overlap except in cases of contingent transgression by turbulent priests or unwarranted secular intrusion into the sacristy.

Typical of this view of the matter is an often repeated story which is told in Archbishop William Temple's book *Christianity and Social Order* (London, 1942). In 1926, a group of bishops tried to bring government, coal-owners and miners together in a solution to the coal strike which was taking place in the British coal mines. Stanley Baldwin, the prime minister of the day, thereupon asked the bishops how they would like it if he referred to the Iron and Steel Federation, the mill-owners' organization, the revision of the Athanasian Creed. The bishops, we are told, were not heard from again.

In the sixty years since then things have changed. In the more recent coal strike of 1985 one of the most vociferous critics of the government and of the management of the mines was the Bishop of Durham. The American Roman Catholic bishops have issued authoritative and forceful documents challenging the policy of the Reagan administration on issues of nuclear warfare and the management of the economy. The Reagan administration's own advent to power was greatly assisted by the campaigning of a group of fundamentalist Christian sects known under the umbrella name of the Moral Majority. One of the most recent and most spectacular interventions of churchmen into politics has been the appeal of Cardinal Sin to the faithful to support the revolution which overturned the regime of President Marcos in the Philippines and brought President Aquino to power. The relationships between Church and State are once more a burning topic of discussion in Western-style democracies. But now it is not the imposition of religious tests by governments, but the advocacy of political policies by churchmen, that is the stimulus to debate. And in Latin

America and elsewhere Christian churchmen have not contented themselves with advocating policies from the pulpit: some have taken an active part in revolutionary movements, others have held office in government. Recent Papal discipline seems to have retarded, but not altogether halted, this investment of the Church in politics; and of course the Pope himself, by his actions and perhaps even just by his existence, has had in the political affairs of Poland a role which bears comparison with that of any secular power or superpower.

Mention of Poland brings to mind another change which has taken place in the course of the present century in the dimensions of the Church–State problem. This is the rise of secular ideologies which have presented the same kind of challenge to civil government as was presented throughout the centuries by the Churches. Nazism, Fascism, Marxism when in opposition to government present the same kind of unassimilable grouping of citizens as crusading or millenarian sects once did; when in power, they display the same totalitarian, persecuting intolerance as did governments which saw themselves as having a duty to uphold religious truth, in the eras of the crusades and the inquisition.

Indeed, the problem of the relation between Church and State can be seen as a particular instance of the relationship between ideology and government. For we may define an ideology as a set of ideas which is simple enough to be grasped by ordinary people without technical training, and yet comprehensive enough to offer an explanation of the most important features of human existence and a guide to the most important social decisions. (I am, of course, abstracting from the question whether any ideology in particular is true or false.) In this sense Freudianism, Marxism, and Christianity are all ideologies, whereas relativity and liberalism are not. Within Marxist states the same kind of tensions can develop between the officials of the party and the officials of the State as developed between bishops and kings at a time when the Christian ideology was dominant in the countries of the medieval West.

In contemporary Western democracies the question of the interaction between Church and State formulates itself in the following manner: what is the role of the Church, or of Churchmen, within the political processes of a secular society? To answer the question, within the Western context, it is necessary to make a number of distinctions: what kind of State are we talking about, what kind of Church are we talking about, and what kind of political activity is in question.

The kind of State within which the question poses itself in its contemporary Western form is a state which is neither theocratic nor atheocratic: that is to say, it neither imposes, nor prohibits, any religious activity as such. It is a secular State in that it does not see the propagation of a particular religion is one of its aims, nor does it impose the practices of any particular religion by law: in that sense it is not theocratic. On the other hand, it is not punitively secular; that is to say, it does not forbid religious activity of any kind, precisely as such. Even in Eastern Europe few States have been explicitly atheocratic in this way; in recent times perhaps Albania has come closest to this form of punitive secularism.

Within such a society there are those, both within and without the Churches, who see no role at all for churchmen in politics. There are those, outside the churches, who value a secular society precisely for its secularism: the only way to avoid the divisiveness of religious sectarianism, they claim, is to have a state that is pluralist, tolerant of religion, but free from any religious influence upon the political process. There are those within the Churches who see religion as essentially a matter for the individual, a matter of the interior life of the heart and mind; Churchmen should not, therefore, meddle in politics, and if the faithful take part in politics it is as individuals not as members of Churches.

Whether a liberal, secular society can welcome a political role for the Church clearly depends on what kind of Church is in question. The Italian nationalist Cavour held out the ideal of a free Church in a free State: both the liberal State and the liberal Church which he proclaimed were anathema to the ecclesiastical conservatives who resisted him in mid nineteenth century. But clearly relations between Church and State are at their easiest, within a pluralist society, if the Church in question is itself liberal rather than authoritarian. A liberal protestant Church fits easily into a liberal, democratic society. Preachers can advise their congregations, pastors form the consciences of their flocks; the faithful can listen to sermons, seek moral guidance, read their bibles. There is here no more violation of due democratic process than if they read their newspapers or listen to political commentators on the radio.

Matters become more complicated when we consider Churches which claim greater authority, and Churches which are international rather than local. If Church leaders do not content themselves with giving moral advice, but reinforce it with ecclesiastical sanctions, there is a greater justification for regarding them as unfairly interfering with due democratic process: as when, in certain countries, Catholic bishops have threatened with excommunication those who have voted in referendums in favour of the legalisation of divorce or the decriminalization of abortion. If a Church is not just a community of believers within a particular political society, but a worldwide organization transcending national boundaries, there is more danger of there being a conflict of loyalties between the duty to the state and the duty to the Church: as in the breasts of English Catholics when the Pope sent the Spanish Armada to depose the excommunicated Elizabeth.

Within secular democracies in recent years Churchmen have spoken out not only on issues which directly concern the Churches themselves, but on a wide variety of issues. Some concern the role of the individual and individual groups within the State: the role of the family, the right to work, the nature of education. Some concern the relation between the State and those outside the State, whether these concern cooperation with other States (by trade or aid) or whether they concern confrontation with other States (by sanctions or by war). By what right do members of Churches seek, in this way, to influence political decisions made by secular States?

There are various different titles which Churchfolk may have to speak and campaign on such issues. First, and most obviously, they have the right to speak as individuals, like any other individual in a society; no one is to be disenfranchized by being a member of a religious community. Secondly, again, particular members of Churches, including Church leaders, may have a particular expertise on the issues on which they speak: economic, geographic, strategic, for instance. But in these cases they are not claiming to speak *as* Churchmen – even if, in a particular society, their ecclesiastical position makes it more likely that they will be listened to (as in Britain where a number of Bishops sit as of right in the

House of Lords). We come more closely to the matter when we acknowledge that members of a particular transnational religious community may, in virtue of that membership, be able to judge international political issues from a perspective which is broader than a local national one: they will have links with, and feel empathy with, others besides their own nationals, and while this may lead to potential conflict in wartime it can be a source of international detente as well as international tension in peace time.

Church groups may claim the role of spokesmen for decaying or disenfranchized values, once recognized throughout society but now mainly preserved within particular religious communities. In these cases they will not appeal to any ecclesiastical authority in support of their contentions: they will make use of secular, rational argument which, they will claim, should have weight with all men and women of good will. It is in this way that Catholic bishops in America argue against nuclear-weapon use on the basis of the just-war tradition; it is in this way that in many European countries members of different religious traditions have taken part in debates on the laws concerning divorce, abortion, euthanasia. The moral majority in America is largely drawn from traditions which have hitherto been politically quiescent: activism has been forced on them, they claim, because values of family life and sexual morality which used to be part of the common decencies of society have been under attack from virulent secularism and from lobbies peddling perversity. On issues such as homosexuality and abortion in the United States there has been formed an alliance between conservative Catholics and evangelical protestants which has cut across not only political boundaries, but traditional ecclesiastical ones also.

Perhaps the claim of religious leaders to speak on political matters is most commonly supported on the grounds that they are the spokesmen and guardians of a particular tradition within the society itself: this is particularly so where the religion in question has had a role in the historic formation of the State, or is respected by a significant proportion of the population. Here, in the Christian context, Ireland and Poland are two obvious examples. It is in this area that the role of the Church can both assist most forcefully in strengthening the cohesion of the State, but can also threaten most powerfully the authority of the State's secular government.

Such, then, are various titles by which Churchmen may claim, without any necessary violation of the democratic process, to have a special voice in the political forum of a secular and liberal society. But of course it is not only by word, but also by deed, that Churches may seek to influence the political process. Many Christians believe that the formation of confessional parties, such as the Christian Democrat parties in Italy and Germany, has not been really beneficial either to the States or Churches concerned, and they welcome the fact that in recent years the political mould in each of these countries has been becoming looser and more secular. In general the participation of Churchmen in government risks a confusion of roles, though in cases when a section of the population has been oppressed, the lack of secular leaders of a sufficient degree of education may place a responsibility on clergy to act as political leaders. Just as, in general, the clergy should not take an active part in the government, it seems undesirable that they should take an active part in subversive activity, even when the illegitimacy of the government, or the wickedness of its policies, is such as to justify attempts to subvert it. In England and in the US clergy have been active in the anti-nuclear movement, and this is well within their legitimate sphere: but when they use forms of protest which are illegal, they risk alienating their faithful, and also may convey a false aura of hallowing to the law-breaking in which they engage. In all these cases, the reason why the involvement of clergy seems inappropriate is because of the possible confusion of roles.

For Macaulay was fundamentally right to see the ends of civil government and the ends of religion as distinct. Because I see a much broader role for government, in such spheres as education and health, than he did, or than any nineteenth-century liberal would, I must correspondingly allow a larger measure of overlap between the spheres of the State and the spheres of the Church. But there must be a limit to the overlap, and I would draw the limit by saying that those who hold authority in the one institution should not hold authority in the other.

There are, in fact, as both history and philosophy show, only two ways in which the claims of Church and State can be effectively harmonized. One is in the theocratic society, when Church and State are identical: where a single hierarchy is responsible for both civil and divine government. The other is in the pluralist secular society, where the two governments are kept apart, and the input of religious leaders takes its due place within the democratic process in the manner I have described. A theocratic society can claim legitimacy as a government only to the extent that the religion which it incarnates is willingly accepted by the citizens over which it rules. In a modern world of international communications, where the plurality of conflicting religious traditions meets the eye not only of every traveller, but of every reader, a theocratic society can survive only by being a closed society and turning its back on the international community. It is for secular, pluralist societies to show that the adoption of liberal democracy need not involve the sacrifice of the values which religious men and women hold dear and which theocratic societies pay a heavy price to preserve.

Index